SOUTHERN. GAY. TEACHER.

SOUTHERN. GAY. TEACHER.

RANDY FAIR

atmosphere press

For all my teachers and supporters,
both in the classroom and out.

AUTHOR'S NOTE

The stories in this book are true and reflect the author's memories of the events. Recognizing that people's memories of events can vary greatly, I am aware that others might have seen these events in a different light. Some names have been changed to protect the privacy of the individuals involved. Especially in the case of students, names and details of their stories have been slightly altered in order to protect their identity. The names of some adults and identifying features have been changed or excluded because while I might have seen the actions of these people as homophobic, that might not have been the way the individuals saw themselves. Homophobia, racism, and sexism are often internalized and so may not be apparent even to those who harbor these feelings. I have omitted the name of the school system because these same things could have occurred in any school system. This story isn't about a particular school system or specific teachers. The stories related here are a reminder of the way things were during a particular time period and in some places remain true even today.

In some cases, I have kept the names intact because many of the straight people mentioned in this book were heroic in their acceptance of the LGBTQ community in a time when this stance could have caused them harm. In the same way, many of the LGBTQ people in this book were equally heroic in taking a stand well before most LGBTQ people were out.

PROLOGUE

"Why are you doing this?" asked Lily, the at one time semi-closeted lesbian assistant principal upon reading the manuscript of this book. This was just the most direct example of the same sentiment uttered by many of the teachers I worked with. It never occurred to me that the answer wasn't obvious.

"Is this just to say, I was a gay teacher and these things happened?"

"No, Lily. It's because many of these things are still happening. Don't you think that there are still schools where Gay Straight Alliance groups aren't allowed to form or aren't allowed to participate in the National Day of Silence?"

"Of course, there are."

"Don't you think it would be good for pre-service teachers to read the story of Connie Williams and debate what the lines are between what parts of a teacher's life are private and which are public?"

"Of course. Randy, I have always admired your activism, but I am afraid you are going to get sued. Why are you using the name of the school system? Why don't you change the names of the teachers?"

"I can do that. One reason that I wanted to keep the names is that a lot of these people were very courageous in a time period where most people wouldn't have been supportive. June, for example, showed a lot of courage, and she deserves to have her name used."

"That's true. She was always in the office defending you. She probably wanted to throttle you, but she still stuck up for you nevertheless. And everything you say is true, so I guess it would be hard to sue you, but no one knows who June is. Why do you need to use the names? Whether you use June's real name or not, someone halfway across the country won't know who she is."

"Yes. I guess you're right. I can change the names."

"You know, Randy, you don't know everything about me.

"Of course, I don't."

"I started teaching in 1966, and I was doing a great job. There were a group of teachers who got together on the weekends, and two of us were lesbians. After a few drinks the other lesbian in the group told the others that we were both lesbians. The next week, the principal called me into his office and said, 'It has come to my attention that you are someone who engages in unnatural acts. I have polled the faculty, and they don't want you on staff. I will give you a good reference, but you have to resign.' I resigned and moved to the state where my partner lived and had to start my teaching career over. It wasn't just about starting my career over. It was about being forced to leave my home and my family. In essence, I became a displaced person."

This story reminded me of the differences I had over the years with the LGBTQ teachers who were slightly older than me. They came from a generation of people who had to hide who they were. I came out in the mid-eighties, during the time of ACT-UP, The Lesbian Avengers, and Queer Nation. While the older generation's silence was infuriating to me, my willingness to speak up was just as annoying to them. From their point of view, my actions, although to me more restrained than I would have liked, were to them a threat to their very existence.

The conversation with Lily also brought back to me the memories of all the times I found myself in a principal's or assistant principal's office trying to defend myself from charges that I thought were unfounded. As troubling as these meetings were for me, I was probably better prepared for them than most people would be. I had been an outsider for as long as I could remember.

Being gay while growing up in Weaver, Alabama was just one of many things that made me feel different from everyone around me. The town, located just outside Anniston, Alabama in Calhoun County, is a part of the foothills of the Appalachian Mountains chain. Weaver at the time I grew up was a town of around 2,000 people. The downtown area of Weaver was marked by the town's one red light at the four corners of two streets. The businesses on the four corners were a produce stand, a gas station, and two churches.

One of the many things that set my family apart from others in the region was our grandmother, the area's most famous bootlegger, Hatie Ward. Calhoun County was a dry county, and my grandmother would drive to Atlanta to purchase the alcohol she would sell illegally. Owning a large parcel of land on a hill and surrounded by a ten-foot redwood fence, my grandmother would hide the alcohol underneath the stairs going to the second floor of her house. This was in a time period when wood paneling was popular, and the stairs were enclosed with the paneling. The panel on the end would slide in and out to provide access but still keep the alcohol hidden from the police. Growing up, my brothers, cousins, and I were trained how to behave when the police showed up. We were instructed that when the police arrived, we should look at the barn and look frightened. The police always searched the barn thoroughly and only gave a cursory look through the house.

Our grandmother's unusual profession also contributed to our strange family structure. My mother was a single mother in a time period when that was practically unheard of. At age 14, she met my father, one of my grandmother's customers. My mother quickly agreed to marriage, and by the time she was in her early twenties, she had four children and my father was in prison.

In addition to all of the strangeness of my family background was the fact that we were one of only two Catholic families in Weaver, Alabama. After my mother's divorce from my father, she married a soldier from nearby Fort McClellan, and we moved to New Hampshire and converted to Catholicism. When my mother's marriage to the soldier failed, we moved back to Alabama, and my mother relied on welfare and charity from the Catholic Church until she could get back on her feet. Because of the help she received from the Catholic Church, my mother was devoted to the religion despite the fact that she wasn't allowed to take communion since she was divorced. While I was angry at the church for its treatment of my mother, I still felt that I had to defend it from the other people in the town who thought that it was a heretical religion. At school, I would frequently have students from the other denominations tell me that they prayed for our family at their church.

Even in my own family, I was somewhat of a misfit. My brothers never seemed phased by our poverty, different religion, or any of the other details of our family life that made us unusual. Their participation in the traditional Alabama pastimes and rituals made it possible for them to fit in despite all these unusual details. They were constantly engaged in hunting and fishing, playing sports, and riding motorcycles. The fact that I never excelled at or liked these activities made me a strange character even to them.

GAY ISSUES IN MY HIGH SCHOOL

Perhaps my career as an English teacher partially came about because one of the only places I received any validation of my gay identity was in high school. This is not to say that all of my high school experiences were positive; most were not. However, I didn't experience the harassment that many LGBTQ teens encounter. Weaver High School in the late 1970s was very small. There were a total of eighty students in my graduating class, and so we were, for the most part, a comparatively close group. Everyone knew everyone, and having some of the most popular students in the school for older brothers didn't hurt.

Any topics regarding sexuality very rarely came up in the classroom and weren't even a huge part of conversations outside of class. Surprisingly for the decade of the seventies, we weren't very liberated, and even when people did talk about sex, the subject of homosexuality rarely came up. The few times I had heard of gay people had always been in hushed tones and always in a negative light. One of the few times I heard anyone in my family discuss the subject was when one of my brother's friends had decided to hitchhike across country. When he returned, I remember him telling my brother about all the men who had given him rides and then had wanted to have sex with him. He told this story in utter astonishment that such a thing could happen. This account was typical of what I had heard growing up, and it had always been a story that depicted the gay man as predator.

Even when I had been much younger, my grandmother had warned my brothers, cousins and me that we should be careful when walking to the Boy's Club. The Boy's Club was a facility meant to keep poor kids off the street. It provided sports, a library, and a community room and had activities to keep the boys busy during the times they weren't in school. We had to cross the railroad tracks to get there, and my grandmother warned us that men hid out around the tracks waiting to grab little boys. I also remember a discussion my mother had with one of her friends when they learned that someone at nearby Fort McClellan was gay. Both my mother and her friend went into great detail describing how disgusting they found homosexuality to be.

This negative view of LGBTQ people as predators was

not confined to Alabama. Anita Bryant, former singer, former Miss Oklahoma, and spokeswoman for the Florida Citrus Commission, began her "Save Our Children" campaign to crusade against LGBTQ rights during this time. The nation for a brief moment became fascinated with Bryant, and she used her celebrity to denounce homosexuals for their "deviant" lifestyle.

The prevailing assumption at that time, at least from the conversations that I overheard, was that men who were gay made this choice because they were too unattractive to get a woman. It is still humorous to me how this stereotype of gay men completely reversed itself in such a short time.

Because discussions regarding lesbians and gays were so rare in my world, it left me feeling as if I were the only gay person in the world that surrounded me. As an avid reader of The Anniston Star since I was extremely young, one might think that I had been exposed to the gay movement that was emerging in large cities. This was the time of Harvey Milk and Fire Island. However, I don't remember until well into high school ever reading anything about homosexuality in the news that didn't depict homosexuals as predators. I certainly never heard anything about the subject of homosexuality in the school's official curriculum.

Even though the curriculum didn't provide any place for me to become aware of the contributions of LGBTQ people, three of my teachers, without planning to, provided me with small moments of hope that I would cherish throughout my life. For someone who felt completely isolated by my growing awareness of my homosexuality, any small, seemingly insignificant event could take on greater meaning.

The first glimmer of hope occurred when I was in the eighth grade (our high school included grades seven through twelve), and a new teacher was hired. When I saw Mr. Fincher for the first time, I, like everyone else, thought he was extremely handsome. I was assigned to his history class. I couldn't have been happier. After a couple of weeks in the class, I was completely enamored. It wasn't anything specific that captivated me. It was just his quiet confidence and his command of the classroom that made him seem somehow greater than other people I had known. Mr. Fincher was assigned to sponsor student council, and I immediately decided to enter the race to be a representative. Luckily for me, no one else was interested, so I won the election.

This gave me numerous opportunities to be around Mr. Fincher. Certainly, I would never have even considered broaching the topic of homosexuality with him, but not long after he started teaching, several rumors began circulating regarding him. The two most prominent rumors spanned the possible extremes. One of the rumors was that he was having an affair with one of the female teachers. The other rumor—and the one that I longed to believe—was that he was a gay man. I can't remember exactly how the idea that Mr. Fincher might be gay was expressed because the topic of homosexuality was extremely taboo. Probably people intimated that he wasn't attracted to women or that he was unnatural. These were the ways gay identity was expressed at the time.

I never did know whether or not Mr. Fincher was homosexual, but just the possibility that he might be gave me hope. If Mr. Fincher could be homosexual, I reasoned, then homosexuals must not be so bad. At Christmas time, Mr. Fincher hosted a party for the student council at his home. Normally, I didn't attend many after school events, but the possibility of seeing more of Mr. Fincher's personal life was too tempting to pass up. I was in awe at the number of books he owned. If Mr. Fincher wasn't homosexual, he certainly fit the category that so many of us were grouped into at that time: "different."

Just as I had seen Mr. Fincher's love of books at his house, in class I had seen his love of knowledge. This was affirming for me for reasons beyond my gay identity. Most of the people around me didn't love reading or knowledge the way I did. In Alabama, education was frowned upon by many of the people around me more often than not. Southerners often felt that an ambiguous group vaguely classified as the "educated class" was trying to impose its will on the regular people. George Wallace won elections by railing against the "pointy headed intellectuals." There was a disdain for any kind of knowledge that couldn't be classified as common sense. One of the few exceptions was my mother. She loved to read, and a frequent excursion for the two of us was a trip to the used bookstore or the public library. However, even my mother found my love of reading a little unusual, and she would frequently chastise me for spending so much time inside the house reading instead of being outside playing sports with my brothers. A son who would rather be inside reading just wasn't what a normal boy should be. Seeing Mr. Fincher's book collection only made me want to read even more and affirmed for me that there were people who admired the knowledge that could be gained from books.

I was also enamored by Mr. Fincher's athleticism.

Every day on my bus ride home I would see him jogging with a member of the football team. Although it wasn't very likely, in my desire to believe that another gay man existed, I hoped that the two of them were dating. Here was an intelligent, athletic, good looking man, and in my mind it was very possible that he might be gay. This was the antithesis of everything the culture had made me believe.

With all of the negative stereotypes I had grown up with, my hope that Mr. Fincher was gay was so strong because that would go a long way towards dispelling those myths about gay men that I had grown up hearing. Mr. Fincher left Weaver High as inexplicably as he had come. I never knew why he chose to leave after a few years, but I do know that those few years had a lasting impact on my life. Mr. Fincher gave me a glimpse that something better could be out there for me.

Years later, when I was in college and trying to decide on a career path, one of the biggest factors in my decision was the hope that I might serve the same role for someone else as Mr. Fincher had for me. Back then, even the smallest incidents, even if not proven, provided hope.

Another teacher that had perhaps an even greater impact than Mr. Fincher was Connie Williams. Mrs. Williams was a controversial figure in the school. In fact, I am not sure that her behavior would have been tolerated in a more conservative decade, but it was the seventies, after all. To understand Connie Williams and her role in the school system, one has to understand just how different that time period was.

While what was considered radical thinking about

some subjects permeated the culture, Weaver, Alabama resisted these new ideas in every way possible. Still, national media brought us any number of new ways of thinking. The war in Vietnam and Watergate had made us question government, the president and authority figures in general. With the television characters Mary Richards and Maude, we were rethinking the role of women in society. The television show, *All in the Family*, was making us question many of the prejudices that had been such a normal part of our way of life. Popular music also was saturated with this new thinking. Helen Reddy's "I Am Woman," Three Dog Night's "Black is Black," and Bo Donaldson and The Heywoods' "Billy Don't Be a Hero" dealt with issues of war, women's oppression and race relations.

In my family, every Sunday was devoted to the popular television show *Sixty Minutes*. This show featured a segment at the end with one liberal and one conservative opining on a controversial subject. I started to realize that I always agreed with the woman who gave the liberal side of the issue, and I was quickly giving up many of the ideas I had been raised with. I had taken down the Confederate flag that had dominated my room for so long, and I became ashamed of George Wallace, rather than proud of him.

These changes in society at large were evident in the school system as well. People were somewhat more open minded about what education was and the topics it should deal with. We experimented with everything. My high school had just been built, and it reflected the liberal educational ideas of the time. The outside was very modern in style, and inside, the classrooms reflected one of the most unusual educational philosophies that has perhaps ever been imagined. Scholars of education had theorized that students were easily bored and would benefit from hearing what went on in other classes, and they proposed open classrooms. With this in mind, we had only a carpet hanging between each classroom, and one wall was nonexistent as it merged with the hallway. Our classes were also a reflection of this new thinking. We were offered classes with names like "Comics as Literature" and "Song Lyrics as Poetry." Connie Williams was at the forefront of these new ideas in education. Although I am sure many parents disapproved of her, her very presence was enlightening to me.

Everything about her was something that set her apart from our other teachers. First of all, she was younger than most and extremely beautiful. She wore the skirts that were fashionable at the time that had a slit in either the front or the side. When she would sit on the edge of her desk, a beautiful leg would be mostly exposed. She was physically fit in a time period when it was almost unheard of for someone to work out at a gym. Her husband took this even further with his bodybuilder physique, and I heard rumors that Mrs. Williams had breast augmentation. Although unlikely, I also heard rumors that she entered wet t-shirt contests at the local bar. Often on Mondays, she wore sunglasses to school, and some students said that this was because she had smoked so much marijuana during the weekend that she wanted to hide her bloodshot eyes.

Mrs. Williams' class was one of those classes where students felt free to discuss everything and knew that they could ask her anything. We often had days where we were allowed to read works of our own choosing. During one of these reading days, I was reading *The Defense Never Rests* by F. Lee Bailey when I came across the words, cunnilingus and fellatio. I went up to Mrs. Williams' desk and asked her what the words meant. Without batting an eye, she explained to me the meaning of both words as if they had been any other word in the English language. She showed absolutely no shock that I was asking this question.

Mrs. Williams was just as unflappable with her opinions in class. Controversial subjects always came up, and she didn't hesitate to deal with them. She could anger students more than any other teacher in the school, but secretly even the students who got angry with her still loved her.

For me, the most significant event that took place in Mrs. Williams' class took place on a seemingly normal day while we were reading *Julius Caesar*. We listened to scenes from the play on a record player, and Mrs. Williams would periodically stop to go over the meaning of the scene. A significant moment in my life took place when a football player raised his hand to ask:

"Why does he sign his letter, 'Thy lover, Artemidourous'?"

"Many of the Romans were bisexual," was Mrs. Williams' nonchalant reply.

"That's disgusting," said the boy who asked the initial question.

"Why do you think that's disgusting?"

"It just is."

I sat there dumbfounded as this discussion continued. As fascinated as I was by where this conversation was going, I was also afraid to let anyone else know how interested I was.

"I don't think that it's disgusting. The Romans had a different way of life than we do," Mrs. Williams went on. "When I was in college at Auburn, my roommate was a lesbian. I didn't think she was disgusting."

"Weren't you afraid?"

"Why would I have been afraid?"

"She might have looked at you when you were undressing."

"If she looked at me and thought I was beautiful, I would be just as happy as if a man looked at me and thought I was beautiful. I know who I am, and I am comfortable with my sexuality, so I am not concerned with anyone else's."

This classroom discussion was another pivotal moment in my life. As powerful as it was that I thought Mr. Fincher might be gay, that was strictly hypothetical. Here was a heterosexual adult willing to have this discussion. She had nothing to gain and in fact much to lose if parents had become angry about this kind of frank talk. Not only was she willing to have the conversation, she was unequivocal in her support of her gay former roommate. In a community that didn't offer any support, every small moment was huge, and this was one of the biggest.

Another couple of incidents that took place in Mrs. Williams' class stick out in my memory. She frequently used a variety of sources for her instruction. One day we might be reading classical literature, and the next we might be analyzing the lyrics to a popular song or a comic. Magazines were a big part of our class, and two incidents occurred both involving *Time* magazine.

Many times, we had to search these magazines looking

for specific types of articles. On one of these searches, I discovered a little blurb, not even an actual article, about some event that was taking place in New York. As a political statement, Jane Fonda had taken a gay couple as her escort. This was most likely not a hugely significant event to Jane Fonda and certainly not a significant story for the magazine, but it was hugely important to me. The idea that someone famous was willing to support gay people made me a little less ashamed of my identity.

Until I saw that small article, I had never read anything that directly mentioned modern-day lesbian or gay people. It is almost impossible to understand now, but to my knowledge, gay people just didn't exist in my world. I was always looking for any small thing that might affirm my existence, and I had been this way all throughout my adolescence. As a reader, I was constantly looking for any glimmer of hope that gay people did exist and did live happy and successful lives. Unable to find it, I transformed the things I read about other people's struggles. I was constantly looking for the downtrodden character who overcame his or her experiences and triumphed in the end.

Another *Time* magazine article that I discovered in Mrs. Williams class showed me for the first time that there were gay people actually engaged in a struggle to make a place for themselves in society. To the best of my memory, it was titled "The Twinkie Defense." In this editorial, the author was decrying the fact that Dan White was acquitted of the murder of Harvey Milk and George Moscone. This was long before Milk became an icon of the LGBTQ community, and this was the first time I had ever heard of Harvey Milk. While it was good to see someone in print decrying the murder of a gay man, the article was for me a double-edged sword. The death of this gay man who had been so open about his homosexuality served as a reminder to me of the dangers of being open about my own sexuality. If Dan White (the man who murdered Milk) could be convicted of manslaughter rather than murder in part because of a claim that he had eaten too much junk food, then I could be quite sure that the life of a gay man was not valued. Clearly this was what happened to gay people who were vocal about their identities. This article reinforced many of my fears about what might happen to someone who was openly gay, but there was an unexpected good side to my finding this story. Like the article about Fonda, this article showed me that there were places where gay people actually did have a community. This statement seems like hyperbole in today's culture of a mass media, but there was really no way for me to find out more about Harvey Milk or about the emerging gay communities in San Francisco and New York. I had very little exposure to the world outside of Weaver, Alabama. In my mind, I knew from these two articles that lesbians and gay men might exist in New York and San Francisco, and I imagined that there might even be a handful in Atlanta, but I didn't think they existed anywhere around me.

Even though I was a constant reader of *The Anniston Star*, I never saw anything in the paper about Milk's election to the Board of Supervisors, and I can only speculate that it was never covered by the news media in Alabama. I did occasionally hear about gay people when they appeared on *The Phil Donahue Show*. In fact, every time I saw that the show would be about gay people, I would fake an illness so my mother would let me stay home, and I could secretly watch the program. While I was drawn to these very few episodes of the show, the reason gay people were on the show to begin with was because their very existence was controversial. While I watched with eagerness, the sensationalism of the program only affirmed for me that gay people were considered freaks by the overwhelming majority of people.

If I had tried to research information about LGBTQ people, I would have most likely been unsuccessful. At that time, any information regarding sexuality required special permission from a librarian. Books about homosexuality were kept in a special section that wasn't accessible to the average reader. If I had known about the existence of these works, I would never have had the courage to ask for them since asking for articles about homosexuality would have made me suspect.

These few examples of the existence of other gay people were fleeting, and it wasn't until my senior year when I was provided with a literary role model. My senior English teacher, Billie Bryan became, like Mrs. Williams, one of my favorite teachers. Her daughter, Missy, was a friend of mine, and Mrs. Bryan was in many ways the antithesis of Connie Williams. Mrs. Bryan represented all of high culture as far as I was concerned. She had white-blonde hair that was always perfectly coifed. Her clothes never had a flaw, and she wore a distinct perfume that filled the room. She represented the epitome of sophistication and class. Here was a woman who knew all of the great classics of literature, all the grammar rules, and the meaning of more words than anyone I knew. She was as traditional as Connie Williams was radical.

Several of us gathered in her room each morning before school. While we mainly did it to talk with our friends, I realize now that we chose her room because of how we felt about her. To me, her words were words of enlightenment, and although I probably didn't seem attentive, I always listened to her every word both in class and out of class. I still look on Mrs. Bryan with amazement. Despite the fact that she was teaching country kids who didn't have an appreciation for the classics, she pressed on. She not only taught these works, but she had every expectation that we would read and understand them.

It was towards the end of the school year when I had my epiphany in Mrs. Bryan's class. In spring semester, she did what she did every year. She broke us into two groups. She informed us all that if we intended to go to college, we needed to learn how to do a research paper. However, she told us that she understood that many people in the class didn't plan on going to college. She offered two choices. Those who wanted to go to college could go to the library every day for two weeks and work on the research paper. Those who didn't intend on going to college could stay and read *The Importance of Being Earnest.*

By this point, I was somewhat sure that I would at least attempt college, but I also loved reading and literature. Despite my appreciation of Billie Bryan's sound judgment, I decided that I would stay and read the play. Like most teenagers, I wanted to take the easy way out.

In one of perhaps the few examples of this, the easy way turned out to be the best for me. On the first day of class while she was introducing the play, Mrs. Bryan told us that Oscar Wilde was a homosexual. This elicited some strong comments from students in the class. These comments were very similar to some of the comments that were aired in my tenth-grade year during the discussion of *Julius Caesar* in Mrs. Williams' class. Mrs. Bryan wasn't bothered by this. She went on to explain to the class that many of the best writers in history were homosexual. She didn't give us the names of these writers, but she did say that we should have respect for the work of these authors. She also made it clear that the homosexuality of the author was not something that would lead her to disparage a work of art.

After this discussion, I rushed the next morning to the library to read the encyclopedia entry on Oscar Wilde. Much to my disappointment, while *The World Book Encyclopedia* did openly state that Oscar Wilde was a homosexual, it also went on to describe his arrest, imprisonment, and eventual death that ensued when he admitted his homosexuality. It gave me pride to know that someone was able to openly identify as gay, but it also offered me another cautionary warning. As sad as it now sounds, I would return to the library frequently to reread this entry.

These brief moments of positive reinforcement helped me make it through the difficult adolescence that most LGBTQ people of my generation faced. My experience in high school was made more palatable by these very few teachers who became role models for me. It also didn't hurt that Weaver High School was so small and close-knit. While most of the students, teachers and members of the community were narrow minded, they still looked out for their own. They might have found me to be a strange young man, but nevertheless, I was still a part of their community, and in their minds, this meant that they had to accept me. Having Connie Williams, Billie Bryan and Mr. Fincher for teachers definitely gave me some comfort at the time and some hope for the future.

Interestingly, none of these incidents that were so important to me had been on a lesson plan. They all occurred as a part of the natural progression of the course and happened because the teachers had created a space where discussions and conversations could happen organically. I spent numerous hours in all three of these teachers' classes and learned many things that would help me academically as I left high school and entered college. But it was these "lessons" that lasted only minutes that would serve me most as I entered a college setting that would prove to be about as stringent in enforcing "compulsory heterosexuality" as my small town had been.

JSU

After graduating from high school, like most of the students from our class who actually enrolled in college, I began my freshman year at nearby Jacksonville State University. Although I knew that I was gay, in 1980 it wasn't something I talked about with anyone or really even accepted myself. Most of my years at JSU were consumed with staying so busy that I didn't have time to think about my identity as a gay man. Besides taking classes, I joined a fraternity, wrote for the student newspaper, and appeared in a couple of plays. In addition to that, I worked part-time in a variety of jobs that included bartending, waiting tables and working at a fast food restaurant.

Like many in my generation, it was the drama department where I discovered a gay community for the first time. Besides the fact that many of the male students involved in the drama department were openly gay, there were also gay professors. One of these professors was one of my favorite teachers at the school, Steve Whitton. I think I knew on some level that Dr. Whitton was gay. I think many others sensed it as well, but it wasn't something we discussed during that time period. Even without coming out openly, Dr. Whitton provided me with a valuable role model of what an adult gay man could be.

I also had a great deal of support from a heterosexual professor and the sponsor of the student newspaper, Opal Lovett. Mrs. Lovett was probably one of the most fascinating and tolerant people I had ever met. Her love of literature made her completely accepting of different ways of living. When one of my friends nervously decided to come out to her, her reply was a brief, "I sort of thought you were gay." It was apparent to him that it didn't make a difference to her one way or another.

I think most of the professors at JSU were to varying degrees accepting, but there was one prominent exception in my experience at the school. Unfortunately for me, this professor was a member of the education department and taught one of the required classes. After going over the syllabus on the first day, he stopped the class, and let us all know that if he discovered any of us were "faggots," we would immediately be given a failing grade for the course. He assured us that teaching was not an appropriate field for someone who was "queer." He actually used these words in the class. As evidence of the degeneracy of homosexuals, he pointed out several men's rooms throughout the campus that had graffiti advertising for sexual encounters. He went on about the mental instability of someone who would look for sex in that way and said that this was proof of the immorality of homosexuals and proof that they were unfit to be teachers. Whether his fears extended to lesbians I couldn't be sure, since he focused all his attention on gay men.

In later years, I might have protested against this rant. Being in part a journalism major, I might have had tools to combat this type of misinformation. However, at the time, that thought would have never occurred to me, and looking back, it is probably fortuitous that it didn't. I am sure the university would have supported the professor's right to voice this opinion, and I am sure that some of the administrators at the school would have shared that same opinion.

At that time in my life, I was not secure enough in my own identity to take on the homophobia of others. I was still working on combating my own internalized homophobia. I felt that my only recourse was to remain silent and wait for graduation, so that I could move to Atlanta and hopefully find a place where I could live a happy life as a gay man.

OAK GROVE HIGH SCHOOL

Because Atlanta was the closest big city and because I knew that there was a community of gay men and lesbians there, I moved the morning after my graduation from JSU. This was 1986 during the end of the conservative Reagan years. The so-called Moral Majority had helped put Reagan in office and had set the tone for a return to a very conservative Christian national mood. Still, in large cities across the country gay communities were beginning to gain in strength and numbers. In these "gayborhoods" LGBTQ people could find solace and comfort. Because Atlanta was surrounded by a plethora of counties with their own school systems, I had the advantage of separating my personal life as a gay man from my career as a teacher. While there were times when the two identities merged, for the most part they remained separate.

When I interviewed with the principal of the school that would ultimately be my first teaching assignment, Mr. Stevens explained to me that Oak Grove was a rural community with very little connection to the city of Atlanta, and since the students weren't surrounded with a lot of diversity, he liked to provide this diversity as much as possible through the teachers. He explained that boys often preferred math classes, and so he often looked for female math teachers to challenge that stereotype. Since English was often seen as something for girls, he liked to find men to teach English classes.

Gay issues just didn't come up at Oak Grove, partially because of the time period where sexuality wasn't really talked about in school, and partially because of the location. Being far removed from the closest major city, LGBTQ people were invisible. I never had a student at Oak Grove come out to me. There was another gay man at the school, the assistant principal, but even though he had been at the school for years, his identity as a gay man was treated more as an open secret.

The only political/social problem I ever had at Oak

Grove was due to the fact that I wasn't a Christian. One day in class, a story that involved a discussion of heaven and hell led a student to ask me if I was a Christian. When I replied, "No," the news spread throughout the student body. Throughout the rest of the day, someone in every class asked the same question. The next day Mr. Stevens called me into his office. He handed me a list of six parents with their phone numbers. He told me that these parents had called him the previous day. He also said that he could take care of it, but that he thought it would be better for me to take care of it on my own. This struck a little fear into me because even as a new teacher, I knew that a few parents could have an incredible impact, and because in 1988 we were still in the midst of the moral majority's power, I knew that there could be serious backlash to a non-Christian teacher. I called each of the parents, and I simply told them that their children were going to leave Oak Grove someday, and they would enter a world full of people who weren't Christians. I told them that this would be an opportunity for these children to learn how to deal with people who are different so they would be better able to deal with it in the future. All the parents accepted this explanation, and while it continued to come up in discussions in my classes at Oak Grove, I never got another call from a parent about it.

I spent most of my time at Oak Grove learning how to be a teacher in general, rather than dealing with how to be a gay teacher. The only thing that could even remotely be related to dealing with gay issues at school was the sympathy I developed with the black students. These students were as much outsiders at the school as I was. Oak Grove's student body was only about twenty percent black. Oftentimes, there would only be one black student in the class.

When I started teaching the Harlem Renaissance, I was somewhat lost. At Weaver High in the late 1970s, we never had a unit on the Harlem Renaissance. I can't even recall reading the works of any black writers in class. I didn't even know how to pronounce the writers' names much of the time. I would notice that when we would read works by African-American authors, the black students would avert their eyes, looking down towards their desks rather than out to other class members. I could see that they worried that the literature would bring attention to their otherness. They wanted to blend in with the other students, and this literature often reminded them of their status as outsiders and made the other students even more aware of their ethnicity.

As the unit went on, and we read "Theme for English B" the black students started to raise their heads up. The juxtaposition of the black student pointing out to the white teacher that they both were learning from each other may have struck a chord. It was also impossible for me to read this poem with students without visibly tearing up. I think the black students could see that I had respect for these black writers. I started to bond with the black students in ways that I hadn't previously, and although I really loved the white students just as much, the connection I had with black students was somehow very different. The black students seemed to have a great deal in common with me. I could sense their anger at the injustices of the world, and most white students just couldn't relate to that feeling.

This sense of being different was something I let the students come to understand through the way I taught.

Even if I had wanted to come out, it would have been inadvisable at that time. In the late 1980s, an openly gay teacher in a Southern state would almost certainly have been fired.

On the rare occasions when my two worlds came into conflict, it was always with adults at the school. One incident that came up involved several young teachers at Oak Grove who had bonded together because of our age and the fact that we were all new teachers. They were constantly wanting to "fix me up" with one of their girlfriends. I immediately began spending time with one of these women, Susan. Susan had the same boyfriend that she had since college, and because her boyfriend's job prevented him from going to extracurricular activities with Susan, we would attend most of these activities together.

I had known Susan almost two years when one day after a baseball game, Susan asked: "I know you go out a lot. What bars do you go to?"

"Susan, you wouldn't know any of them," I replied. I was surprised when Susan got her feelings hurt because she thought I was implying that she wasn't knowledgeable about nightclubs.

She said, "You know, Randy, I don't just sit home every night. I know some of the clubs." When I started naming some of the clubs, she said, "I haven't heard of any of those." When I mentioned Backstreet, she had heard of it. "That's a gay club, isn't it?" she asked.

"Yes," I casually replied.

She quickly followed up, "Are you gay?"

I didn't intend to back out after going this far, and I said, "Yes."

Susan was hurt when she asked, "Why didn't you tell me?"

I tried to explain the situation by saying, "I didn't know when a good time to tell you would be. What am I supposed to do? Pass the salt, and by the way, I'm gay?"

Susan agreed that she wouldn't have known how to bring it up either. We became even closer after I told her. More importantly, after Susan knew, I felt that I had to tell June, my department chair. June had helped me so much that I didn't want her to think that I trusted Susan with this information, but I didn't trust her. When I called June to tell her, she let me know that she had already figured it out. Over the years, June and I would frequently say that she did for me on the issue of feminism what I had done for her on the issue of LGBTQ rights. I believed in feminism before I met June, but after meeting June, I had a person to associate with those beliefs. In the same way, June believed in LGBTQ rights, but now the issue became even more personal for her.

I also depended on June's support when I wrote my first letter to the editor of a gay magazine. There had been a column in Etc. magazine that I found to be insulting to most gay men. The column was about the importance of monogamy, and the writer expressed his opinion that if we all just formed monogamous relationships, then the rest of the country would accept us. I felt compelled to write in and refute this ridiculous idea. In my opinion, the attitude the writer was espousing was the same attitude that LGBTQ people often used to attack other members of the community: basically this argument asserted that if we could all be conservative and "respectable," people would accept us. I wanted people to see that we should stick together and try not to judge others in the community. Our judgmental attitude towards other LGBTQ people was as bad to me as mainstream society's judgement of us. I was completely surprised when my letter, although severely edited, was published. When I wrote it, I didn't even think about the implications of a teacher writing something that would defend promiscuity and diverse ways of forming relationships.

June later told me that she was at a party where the letter was discussed by several teachers. Apparently, only other LGBTQ teachers or people who were supportive of LGBTQ people saw the letter, so no controversy ensued. June was completely supportive of my initial effort to be a part of the larger conversation going on in the community. This would just be the first of many times that June would have to defend my right as a teacher to express a public opinion.

RIVERSIDE HIGH SCHOOL

After only three years at Oak Grove, the school closed. The county was undergoing a major consolidation project. In the early 1990s, most of the research supported the idea that larger schools were better. The theory was that in a larger school more high-level advanced classes could be offered. For example, at a small school there might not be enough students to offer Advanced French or Advanced Latin, but at a larger school there would be more students wanting to take these courses, and students could get more out of the high school experience if a wider variety of classes were offered.

No one ever stopped to think about the psychological benefits of small schools. In that time period, the idea of a close community experience was so taken for granted that the people at the top didn't think about the effects that losing this sense of community would have for the students. In addition to this, the powers in the central office didn't think about the culture of each individual school. Oak Grove was a very rural school, and it would be merging with Campwood High School. Campwood High School was much larger, and while it was somewhat rural, it also had a significant population of urban students. The county had been sued over discrimination issues in the past, and so as part of a solution to this problem, they had developed the M to M program, majority to minority. Under this program, any student who went to a school where students of his or her ethnic background were in the majority could choose to go to a school where the student would be in the minority. Virtually all the M to M students were African-Americans. I never once heard of a white student taking advantage of this opportunity. This program resulted in a sizable number of Campwood High's students being African-American, and they did not live in the community. While there were African-American students at Oak Grove High, the school was so far south that few M to M students applied to come there, and so the African-American students at Oak Grove shared the rural culture of the white students.

When Riverside formed, the school would be fifty/fifty, meaning exactly half of the students would be white and half would be black. This racial split was intensified by the fact that most of the M to M students were from Atlanta and virtually all of the white students were from small towns well outside the city of Atlanta. Tensions arose immediately. The first controversy ensued as soon as cheerleading tryouts were over. All of the students selected as cheerleaders were white, and the fact that not a single African-American made the cheerleading squad that first year naturally created a lot of hostility. The male sports teams had large numbers of African-American students participating, and anyone who was paying any attention at all couldn't help but wonder why there wasn't a single African-American girl deemed qualified to be a cheerleader. It became clear that traditional ideas of beauty were factors in the choice of the cheerleaders, and African-American girls felt they were being denied an opportunity to cheer for people of their same ethnic group. The sexism involved in the idea of girls cheering on boys wasn't a consideration for most of the people involved in this issue, and whenever I brought it up, it was immediately dismissed. People were much more interested in talking about the issue of race than they were of discussing sexism, and there was no recognition of how these issues might be intertwined.

In classrooms, there was also a great deal of segregation. I had never given students an assigned seat as other teachers did in order to keep friends away from each other. My policy had always been that students needed to learn how to behave around their friends so they would be able to develop the maturity they would need to get along in college and other settings. Because the students in my classes could sit anywhere, all the black students would sit on one side of the room, and all the white students would sit on the other. When I thought about this split, it always amazed me that the African-

American students would automatically gravitate towards the part of the room that had posters of famous African-Americans. I always referred to the split as the line of demarcation. When I would point it out to the students, they would all reply, "We want to sit by our friends. There's nothing wrong with it." In the cafeteria, the same thing took place. There were black tables and white tables. Rarely ever did anyone cross this line.

The most popular student in the school was a dark-skinned Jewish student who had extremely curly hair. All of the black students thought he was black, and all the white students thought he was white. He was one of the few students in the school to have many friends on both sides of the racial barrier.

Towards the end of the first year, race riots broke out at the school. The school was featured on the front pages of The Atlanta Journal, and all the local television news stations covered the tension created by the riots. The worst coverage came from the local television news stations. Instead of finding the average black or white student to interview, they looked for the extreme ends of the spectrum. They would interview the white students who were wearing Confederate Flag t-shirts, and they would interview black students who had on Malcolm X t-shirts. Due to the news coverage, the parents were afraid to send their children to school, and for about two weeks, the school virtually shut down. For the first week, there might be two or three students in each class. By the second week, students had gradually started to come back.

This climate was extremely challenging for teachers. I always had to fight the perception that I was favoring one group over the other. The white students would go to the white administrators and say that I liked the black students better than them. The black students would go to the black administrators and say I was prejudiced against them. This same thing happened to virtually every teacher at the school, and most of the students made the most of these claims in order to avoid facing any punishment for breaking the rules.

This atmosphere made it incredibly hard to conduct a lesson. Fights might break out in the halls on any given day, and the entire lesson was lost. Other distractions could come up as well. For instance, on one day when a student went to the restroom, he came back and said, "Mr. Fair there are two sets of feet in that stall." When I went over to see what was going on, a young man ran out of the restroom leaving the girl that he had been having sex with to get caught by me. So much for chivalry.

This was the first time in my teaching career when I had seen this level of dysfunction among my students. I taught two sections of a senior class that was intended for students who weren't planning to go to college. In this class, every female student I had was either pregnant, got pregnant during the year, or already had a child. While they weren't bad kids, they had difficulties I had never imagined a high school student could face.

BRIAN

At the same time that my teaching experience was absorbed with these issues of multiculturalism, the nation was grappling with these issues as well. This was the early nineties, and nothing illustrates this as well as the popular culture of the time. By the end of the eighties, *The Cosby Show*, a show where issues of race were secondary to the plot, had given way to shows, such as *In Living Color*, that dealt with multicultural issues head on. Nike came out with its slogan, "If we're gonna live together, we've got to play together." Rodney King asked us, "Can't we all get along?" And Michael Jackson told us that it "doesn't matter if you're black or white."

Multiculturalism was at the forefront of educational research, but for most schools in my county's school system, this was purely theoretical. The county school system was, and still is, sharply divided by race with the northern part of the county being predominately white and the southern part being predominately black. Oak Grove had been an anomaly in its racial makeup because it was so far to the south of the county. Riverside High became the crucible for these ideas of multiculturalism.

In this climate, things could happen that would be totally unheard of in most suburban schools. The entire time I was at Riverside there was a constant battle between white and black ethnic groups, and as the first few school years went by, more and more white students started withdrawing to go to a private religious school in the area. Suddenly, this atmosphere of multiculturalism brought forth issues I had never dealt with in my teaching experience. One of these situations took place with a student named Brian.

Brian was in the class I taught for students who didn't intend on going to college. I had known him even before he was in my class. He was a friend of a student who had been one of my favorite students when I had taught him in tenth grade. Both of these students were misfits even among the white students. They both embraced an alternative style of dress and behavior.

Brian took this dress to a level well past the level of his friend. Brian came to school each day dressed in Doc Martens and army fatigues. This look had a distinctive meaning behind it. As multiculturalism was making headway across the nation, the inevitable backlash was taking place among a very small number of whites, and the skinhead movement was attracting national attention. There was a manner of dress and music that defined skinhead culture, and Brian affected this persona. Although Brian's dress somewhat indicated that he was a "skinhead," he didn't overtly express any of these views at first.

As I got to know Brian, I started to believe that his manner of dress was his way of intimidating people in advance. Students who don't fit in with the mainstream, are often picked on in schools, and I believed that Brian felt that his clothing gave him a certain level of protection. I liked Brian because he was extremely intelligent, and he wasn't afraid of being different from the other students. Brian knew my views were very different from his because his friend had told him about the things we had talked about in class, but he still gravitated towards me nevertheless.

In the spring semester, he wrote a paper that was full of racist, sexist, and homophobic rants. I didn't know what to do about the situation because he was expressing what he truly believed at the time. I wrote a note on his paper saying, "I disagree with everything you have said in this paper, but the paper is well written." Because it was well written, I graded it only on the basis of grammar and style, and I gave Brian an A for the assignment. I also made a copy of the paper and gave it to the counselor. When I expressed my belief that this paper was a cry for help, the counselor just said, "What do you want me to do about it?" I suggested that some counseling would be in order, but the counselor wasn't interested in something that would take up more of her time.

I always had the students keep their writings in a folder that we locked in filing cabinets. One day while we were in the computer room, Brian forgot to put his folder away. When the next class came in, some black students who were sitting near the computer Brian had used found his folder, and because Brian was such an unusual student, they decided to read what he had written. Perhaps because of the note I put on top of the paper, they chose that paper to read in its entirety.

The black students were understandably very angry. Without my knowledge (I didn't even know they had read the paper), they took the paper out of the room, showed it to other African-American students, and reported it to one of the black assistant principals. Later in the day, she called me into her office. She was infuriated, and she wanted to have me fired on the spot. She accused me of racism, and she wanted to know how I could give a paper like this a good grade. When I pointed out the comment I had written on the top, the fact that I turned a copy into the counselor, and that I was grading it on the quality of writing not on the opinion of the author, this made no difference to her. She insisted that the paper should have been given an F because of the content, and she assured me that she would take this up with the principal.

The paper almost resulted in another race riot.

Throughout the day, the black students were threatening the white students and promising to get revenge on Brian. The students had a common way of attacking students they didn't like. They would form a large group, and when the victim of the attack would come out of the classroom or enter a hallway, one student would trip the victim and get him or her on the ground. The others would encircle the student and begin kicking. This was the plan the students had in mind for Brian.

Although I felt that Brian never should have written that paper, I also felt that the black students violated his privacy by reading his personal thoughts. The administration had to step in to prevent any harm from coming to Brian. The African-American students weren't angry with me because they had seen the note I had written, and by that time, I had established a reputation at the school that precluded anyone realistically depicting me as a racist.

Far from being seen as racist, most of the black and white students thought I took political correctness to an extreme level. One of the early conflicts I was engaged in at Riverside involved race. The school mascot selected for the new school was a native person. I refused to wear anything with the mascot on it. When students would ask me why, I always used the same example. I would always ask them to imagine if the mascot were the Riverside Crackers, and every time the team scored, a white man in overalls came on the field and spat tobacco, or imagine if the mascot were the Riverside Slaves, and every time the team scored, a black man came out and swung a chain. While this always elicited laughter, the students could better understand why the native mascot could be seen as offensive. Students would tell other students in the school about my beliefs, so even students who hadn't had my class knew my political beliefs. This widespread knowledge of my ideas prevented students from thinking I shared Brian's beliefs.

While the students trusted me, the administration did not. At least in part, this distrust was part of the homophobic climate of the school. This homophobia had been made somewhat apparent to me even though it was carried out in a very subtle manner. For example, when one of the assistant principals came to observe my class, he told June, "I was surprised. Randy is really a good teacher." I have to believe that at least part of the reason for that surprise had to do with his belief that a gay teacher was somehow inappropriate. As always, in the case of Brian's paper, June as my department head stepped in to defend me. Some of the administrators still insisted that I be fired for accepting the paper. I tried to point out that the paper was as insulting to me as a gay man as it was to any other group of people since Brian had included paragraphs about his hatred of homosexuals. I also pointed out the fact that I had taken the paper to the counselor and asked that it be dealt with. No one seemed to think the counselor failed to take appropriate action.

As the weeks went on, we continued to worry that Brian's paper would cause the race riots to start again, but luckily, the whole thing blew over. As the years went on, Brian joined the military and abandoned his racist beliefs. The encounters he had in the military, his visits to other countries and his observations of different ways of life had altered the views he once had. I received a letter from him telling me all of this and thanking me for letting him express his opinions, as horrific as they were, without judging him for them. I think that Brian wanted to test these ideas out on a gay teacher. He wanted someone to tell him that his ideas were wrong, but he also wanted someone who wouldn't judge him for expressing these beliefs.

MARY

At Riverside, I faced the struggles of students dealing with gay issues for the first time in my teaching career. One of these involved a girl I will call Mary. Mary had been a student in my tenth-grade honors class. She came to me one morning and asked me if she could ask a question. I said, "Sure, but if it is too personal, I will just tell you I don't want to answer it." I was surprised when she asked me, "Is the Pardoner in *The Canterbury Tales* gay?" This wouldn't have been the question I would expect from a seventeen-year-old student. I answered, "No. I don't think the Pardoner is gay. I think he has been castrated, and that is not the same as being gay, but I will have to look up some research in order to give you evidence of that." I told her to give me about a week. This was way before the internet, so I couldn't research something by simply Googling it. I wasn't sure whether this was some kind of test or not, but as an English teacher, I wanted to show her that I took research seriously. I could have told her to research it herself, but something told me that there was a bigger reason that she wanted my answer on this question. During my planning period, I headed straight for the library.

The librarian was one of the best librarians I have ever seen. That is really saying something because I have never met a homophobic librarian, and the librarians I have met in every school I have worked in have all been exceptional. This librarian would search for hours to find anything a student or teacher needed, and I am sure she would have found the answer if Mary had asked her. However, I think that the same fear that I had in my youth about asking for information about gay topics was also at work with Mary.

In a time when these topics were still taboo, even as a teacher I was a little uncomfortable asking the question. But the minute I asked, we began our search. After a few days with both of us looking, we found the information that would answer her question. I copied the pages with the information so I could have concrete evidence, and I had it ready for her when she returned about a week later.

I gave her the information, and I said, "Here is some evidence showing that the Pardoner should not be considered to be a gay character. Now, I want to ask you something. Why were you so concerned about this?" She replied, "Well, my teacher told us the Pardoner was a gay character, and the Pardoner is such a despicable character that I thought that might mean that he was saying all gay people are like the Pardoner. I haven't told anyone this, but my father is gay." It turned out that Mary was being raised by her gay father and his partner.

While I had always assumed that there were probably some students in my class who were gay, this was the first time I had ever thought about the possibility that I might have students who had gay parents. This was during the 1990-91 school year, and gay parents were virtually unheard of at that time. This incident also made me realize why these issues were so important. Here was a student who was being raised by a gay couple, and yet the only representation in literature that she had ever seen of a gay man was the Pardoner in *The Canterbury Tales*, a character that actually was not gay at all.

I suddenly realized why she brought her question to me. While I would like to think she admired my scholarly skills, it is much more likely that she knew I wouldn't support the negative stereotyping of gay people. I made it clear to her that her teacher most likely didn't mean to disparage gay people, but this is probably what he was taught when he read *The Canterbury Tales* in his high school experience. I encouraged her to take the evidence to him and talk with him about it. She didn't want to do that, and I couldn't blame her. At that time, she was most likely one of the only students in the school who had gay parents. However, I hoped that this small piece of research gave her some solace.

STEVEN

This idea that even heterosexual students needed to know about gay issues was further reinforced for me a year later with a student who I will call Steven. Steven was in the senior class for students who didn't intend to go to college. At the time, we even called the class "Non-college Bound Senior English." Steven was a great student and very mild mannered, especially for that class. He never caused any discipline problems.

At the very end of the year, he suddenly started acting out. In the middle of class one day, he said loudly, "I hate faggots." I replied, "Steven, you know you are not allowed to use that word in this class. Don't do that again." The next day, he did the same thing. Once again, it happened almost exactly in the middle of the lesson. I said, "I have already warned you about that, and if you do it again, I am going to turn you in to the administrator."

The third day, he did the same thing, and I turned him into the administrator. Because I knew the administrators were extremely homophobic themselves, I wasn't surprised that the administrator took no action, but I was surprised when Steven made it a point to come in the next morning to tell me that the administrator didn't give him any punishment. When he told me this, I said, "Well, since the administrator didn't give you any punishment, you can just come in for detention with me." I didn't expect him to show up. He was a senior with only two weeks left before the end of the school year. We both knew that if he didn't show up for the detention, nothing would be done.

I was surprised when he did show up on the morning of his detention. He even came early, getting there before I even arrived. Realizing that he wanted to tell me something, I asked him why he continued making those statements when I told him to stop. He said, "You want to know why I hate faggots?" I first said, "Don't keep using that word, and yes, go ahead and tell me." He surprised me with his reply when he said, "My father is a faggot, or as you say a gay man, and he left my mother when I was born to run off with his boyfriend. I haven't seen him in years, and now, he wants to go to my graduation. That's why I hate faggots."

We spent the next thirty minutes talking about his father. While I assured him that it was understandable that he would be angry with his father, I asked him to think about what it must have been like for his father to be gay in the mid-seventies when Steven was born. By the time Steven left, I could tell that while I hadn't solved his problem, he did at least get to talk about it with someone. This is something he wouldn't have been able to tell anyone other than a gay man.

As with Mary, I realized that he deliberately brought up this subject in my classroom because he wanted to have a conversation about it. He could have brought this up in another teacher's classroom, and not only would his comments have been allowed, they would very likely have been supported. He wanted someone to give his father's side of the story. This isn't to dismiss or excuse his father's lack of involvement, but I think that Steven wanted some explanation, and he wanted some movement towards a future where he might be able to forgive his father.

This was another reminder to me that we shouldn't remain silent on these issues, but at that time, I was a little uncertain what to do about this silence. June often referred to me as "the voice crying in the wilderness." The obvious need for discussion around this topic conflicted with the almost tacit conspiracy on the part of the school system and society to prevent any discussion of the topic. I pointed this conspiracy out whenever I got the chance. For example, when the school system was adopting a new literature textbook series, I asked the salesman why none of the lesbian or gay authors were identified as lesbian or gay in their biographies. I pointed out that the biographies of heterosexual authors always listed the partner of the author. The salesman thought I was crazy. He quickly told me, "These textbooks are published in Texas, and we have to appeal to people in Texas since they are one of the biggest school systems in the country. Do you really think anyone in Texas would buy these books if we put that information in there?"

NEVAEH

Even some students who didn't have any personal reason to deal with LGBTQ issues wanted to better understand the LGBTQ culture. Students were becoming more aware of LGBTQ people as more celebrities started coming out, either intentionally or unintentionally. This coming out process was given an unintentional and unfortunate boost due to the AIDS epidemic. Ironically, all throughout the decade of the eighties the tragedy of AIDS had the positive effect of making lesbians and gays more visible to the culture at large. One of the biggest revelations occurred when the public became aware of Rock Hudson's homosexuality after his death from complications due to AIDS. This resulting discussion caused by the revelation of Hudson's sexuality cannot be overstated. Suddenly, people, especially older people, were openly discussing a topic that they had only spoken of in whispers before. As the eighties was coming towards an end, the world of sports, one of the areas that was considered to be the most homophobic, was rocked when Olympic gold medalist Greg Louganis revealed his HIV-positive status in a bestselling biography.

Even though awareness of LGBTQ people was increasing, the subject was often brought up in the most sensationalized ways. In popular culture, LGBTQ people were being used to add a shocking and controversial aspect to whatever was being produced for mass consumption.

Rod Jackson, a model, and Bob Paris, a former Mr. Universe, challenged the public's stereotypes when the two conducted a tour of all the popular talk shows after holding a commitment ceremony. While the two were embraced by the talk show hosts, they were clearly being used to promote a ratings boost. The two were laudable for their courageous coming out story, but they were offered up by the media precisely because they weren't what people expected a gay person to look like. Just as daytime television used LGBTQ people for a sensational effect, nighttime dramas started to use gay storylines to add a salacious element, and a controversy ensued when television's first gay kiss took place on the very popular show, L.A. Law. This gay storyline boosted ratings as viewers wanted to see the controversial kiss, and although this did bring the nation's attention to the fact that LGBTQ people did exist, it reinforced the idea that homosexuality was somehow exotic and scandalous.

A backlash against this increasing visibility on the part of LGBTQ people inevitably took place. The notorious Westboro Baptist church started its assault on LGBTQ culture, and far from appearing extreme, they voiced opinions that were only slightly to the right of most of mainstream culture. Popular songs started featuring homophobic lyrics. This went as far as The Beastie Boys attempts to name an album *Don't Be a Faggot*. Conservative Republicans were starting to realize that berating LGBTQ people was great political strategy. Jesse Helms was increasing his national stature with his homophobic attacks, and Pat Buchanan was just beginning his political attack on the LGBTQ community that would culminate with his 1992 convention speech where he declared a "culture war."

At the very time that LGBTQ people were becoming more visible and gaining some acceptance, there were more and more people voicing their hatred of LGBTQ people. Most of the students at Riverside, both black and white, were deeply religious, and from my point of view it seemed that the churches of virtually every student were openly hostile to LGBTQ people. This only exacerbated the confusion on the part of most of my students. While most of my students liked me as a teacher, they were being told from a variety of sources that there was something about me they should disapprove of and even find evil. Frequently, students would come to school on Monday morning and say that they had prayed for me at their church. This confusion became clearly evident with one student in particular.

While teachers are not "supposed" to have favorite students, there are always some students who make a bigger impact than others. Perhaps there is some reason why these students are more drawn to that particular teacher. This connection between teacher and student is often inexplicable.

One of my favorite students, who later became a personal friend, didn't start off that way. I first taught Nevaeh at Oak Grove High. In the late eighties and early nineties, high school started in eighth grade since there were no middle schools at that time. Being the new teacher, I was assigned to teach the eighth graders. When Nevaeh was assigned to my class, I recognized her name right away. I had taught her brother a couple of years earlier, and I knew her mother from conferences we had regarding her older brother, Robbie. To say that Nevaeh's mother was not a big fan of mine is an understatement. Mrs. Gardener had grown to dislike me tremendously when I taught Robbie. She felt that I didn't understand him. Robbie was an extremely bright, young man full of potential, but impossible to get focused. Mrs. Gardener thought Robbie's problems were somehow my fault.

Like Robbie, Nevaeh was incredibly and naturally bright. Her curiosity made her a great student, but in eighth grade she was far more focused on being the popular cheerleader. While her popularity might have been one of her main concerns, she was still very concerned with her grades, and she wanted to do well in school. When she skipped my class one day to work on the homecoming float, I turned her in to the administrator. This angered Nevaeh, and she planned to take revenge. Since the topic of religion had first come up at Oak Grove, my views on religion were pretty well known at the school. Nevaeh had decided to draw on this controversy and had worked out an elaborate scheme to get me started talking about religion in class and secretly record it. She planned then to use this recording to get me fired. Her hope for this plan relied on a common belief on the part of students that religion is not allowed under any conditions even if it is a part of the literature.

Students told me of the plan, and so I knew what she was doing when she brought the topic up in class. Much to the dismay of the students who tried to warn me, I went on and said the same things I always said about religion. Several students looked fearful as they worried that I was getting myself in trouble. At the end of the class period, I revealed that I knew about the recording, and then I pointed out that teachers are allowed to talk about religion if the topic comes up because of the literature or as a natural part of the class. I used the situation as what is sometimes referred to as a "teachable moment." I explained to the students that teachers are not allowed to try to persuade someone to embrace or reject a religion, but a general discussion of religion was allowed. I didn't identify that I knew that Nevaeh was the one recording the conversation, but I invited the student who made the recording to take it to the administration.

A red-faced Nevaeh came up to the front of the room when the class ended. After everyone left the room, Nevaeh started to explain:

"I'm the one who made the tape of the class."

"I thought you were the one. Why did you do that?"

"I was mad about you turning us in for skipping class. If we hadn't skipped, the eighth grade wouldn't have had a float. We got detention and got in trouble with the cheerleading coach."

"Well, you should have. You did the wrong thing. You are probably the brightest student in the class, and I want you to be here."

"We didn't miss anything important."

"At your age, you are not the one to decide what's important or not. Even if you didn't miss anything important, you have to be a responsible person and do the right thing. If you had asked me, I might have let you go."

"I'm sorry. The next time, I will ask."

Throughout the rest of the year, we had good days and bad days, but Nevaeh always impressed me as one of the brightest students in the class. At the end of the year, Nevaeh was clearly upset one day. When I asked her what was wrong, she explained to me that she was upset because she had to attend the graduation ceremonies that evening because she was in the band. Her distress was due to the fact that graduation that year was on her birthday. Because she had to be at school all day and then perform at graduation that night, her birthday party had to be delayed for the next day.

Without really meaning to, I made a gesture that would change the relationship I had with Nevaeh for the better. There was a group of teachers who commuted from Atlanta to Oak Grove, and we always stayed at school on graduation night because it was pointless to go home and turn right around and come back. We always went to the mall and had dinner. While at the mall, we stopped to look around the bookstore. I just happened on the book, That Was Then, This is Now, and I remembered Nevaeh's birthday. Nevaeh and I were still not close, but I always loved the rebellious kids and was always trying to reach out to them, so I bought a copy for Nevaeh. I remembered how much she had loved The Outsiders when we read it in class, and I knew that she would love to continue reading in the series.

I don't know if was this birthday gesture or something else that created a bond between Nevaeh and me, but when Oak Grove closed, and we ended up at Riverside, Nevaeh started to come sit in my room each morning before school. We would talk as I would prepare for class. Since Nevaeh was so popular, it wasn't long before we had an entire group hanging out in my room each morning.

Towards the end of the year, Nevaeh came in my room

at the end of the day when she knew I would be alone. She said, "I want to ask you something. Are you gay?" This was the first time a student had asked me so overtly. After a few minutes of us going round and round with me asking her what difference it made, and her saying she just wanted to know, I finally decided to give some kind of answer. Since this was the first time a student had ever asked me this question, I didn't know what to say, so I said, "I am not going to tell you that I am not gay because that will make you think that I am ashamed of it. But I am not going to tell you that I am gay because that will get me fired."

Nevaeh accepted my explanation since it was clear to her what the answer was, but after a while I think she got more and more curious. She knew that I volunteered at Project Open Hand, an organization that made meals for people with AIDS, and she decided that she wanted to volunteer there too. I tried to discourage her from volunteering. One of the good things about teaching at one place and living in another was that there was some separation and privacy. But Nevaeh was insistent, and not only did she volunteer there, but she frequently brought football players and cheerleaders to volunteer there as well.

Since at Project Open Hand I always did the job of washing dishes, I worried about Nevaeh working on the assembly line putting the meals together. These assembly lines were full of the gossip of the week, and sometimes the discussions could be pretty frank. I was a little uncomfortable having one of my students volunteering there and overhearing what were sometimes overtly sexual conversations. It would have been pointless to ask the gay men working to watch what they said. Part of the enjoyment they got from volunteering was the social interaction they had while doing the work. Nevaeh insisted on working on the lines, and she and her friends got to hear these men talk about their dates and personal lives. Occasionally, when the talk became too much, Nevaeh would bring her friends back to the dishwashing area, and they would dry the dishes for me.

On one of these occasions, she came back to dry dishes and brought one of her friends, a football player named Cori, with her. They wanted to know what I was doing when our shift was over. I told them that I was going to a book reading, and they decided they wanted to go with me. I told them they couldn't, and they insisted on knowing why. When I finally told them the reading was taking place at a lesbian bookstore, Charis, and the book was *Stone Butch Blues*, a novel by a transgender activist, they insisted on going. I again told them they couldn't go. They informed me that they didn't need my permission to go to a public place, and that they would either go with me or they would go by themselves. I decided that I better just let them go with me so I could at least monitor the situation.

We got to the bookstore, and the football player and I were the only two men in the place. The reading attracted the most extreme feminists and most exclusionary lesbians the community had to offer. We were surrounded by some of the most masculine women I had ever seen. When the woman who was planning to introduce the author got up to check the sound of the microphone, she asked the crowd, "Is this loud enough?" Nevaeh's friend, Cori, yelled out in his masculine voice, "Turn it up."

Everyone in the place turned to look at us. He, of course, didn't know that in this environment his aggressive answer would be viewed as the attempt of a man to assert patriarchal privilege. His face flushed as the women in the audience stared harshly at him.

As the reading continued, both Cori and Nevaeh listened attentively as the author described his experiences as a transgender person. I think both of them were fascinated by the reading and intrigued by both the author and the women in the audience. This was the first time either of them had been around a group of open lesbians.

When the reading was over, I had to explain to Cori why his response was considered inappropriate for most of the audience. I explained to both Nevaeh and Cori that many lesbians, especially at that time, felt that their needs were ignored in mainstream, male-dominated society. I made it clear that this was not true of all lesbians, but some lesbians preferred to separate themselves from the dominant culture in order to have a place where they could assert their own voices. Cori and Nevaeh, who had witnessed the struggles of black students facing similar issues at Riverside, were more prepared to understand this need on the part of some members of minority groups to step away from mainstream society.

On the way back home, Nevaeh and Cori swore each other to secrecy. They both felt that they had transgressed conventional boundaries. At first, I worried about this kind of exposure for Nevaeh, but as the years went on, I came to see how important it was in her development. Nevaeh's mother belonged to an Evangelical church that had views that were seen as extreme even among Christians. Nevaeh was desperately seeking experiences that would take her out of this very narrow world. As I watched Nevaeh grow over the years, I saw just how much her exposure to difference helped her navigate the changes in her views that would take place over the years.

MARY BRYANT

Just as with the students, many of the experiences I had with straight people at the time were heavily influenced by their religious beliefs. The people who were most supportive of me tended to be people who did not have very strong or had no real religious beliefs. Oftentimes, I would deliberately avoid people who seemed to be deeply religious because I assumed they would be homophobic.

One of the people who I often tried to avoid because of her religious beliefs was another teacher in Riverside's English department, Mary Bryant. My first reaction to Mary was not a good one. My main problem with Mary was that frequently at English department meetings she would insist on reading her poetry aloud. Her rhyming couplets were always about the topic of Christianity, and besides finding them maudlin, I felt that they bordered on a violation of the separation of church and state. I never complained to June about them because I reasoned that these were personal expressions of what Mary really felt, and so we should be accepting of her desire to share her artistic expressions with us whether we believed the same thing or not.

I stayed away from Mary as much as I could because I didn't think I could possibly have anything in common with her. It was due to my friend Sophie that I learned that

I had far more in common with Mary than I might have known. Sophie was a fun-loving social studies teacher and close friend of June's. She loved to laugh and make school as fun as possible for both students and teachers. She also liked to play pranks on people. One day, she placed a religious tract in my mailbox as a joke. These tracts were commonly used at the time by religious zealots. This one, as so many of them were, was a cartoon pamphlet warning people about the dangers of hell if they didn't become saved.

When I found the pamphlet, I became convinced that Mary had placed it in my box. Mary had often made religious overtures towards me by asking me about church and telling me about the importance of religion. Without any investigation, I immediately went to Mary's room prepared to confront her with the pamphlet. When I showed it to her and asked if she had put it in my mailbox, she firmly told me to have a seat. It was the first time I had realized what a strong presence she could have when she wanted to.

As soon as I sat down, she said, "I know you think that I don't like you and don't want you here, but let me tell you something. I was the first African-American teacher in an all-white school. Every day I came into class, the students had written 'nigger' and 'nigger go home' all over the board. I know what you go through every day here, and I don't mind at all your being here. I would never put a pamphlet like that in your mailbox. I would come and talk to you about it first."

After apologizing to Mary, I left with my face flushed and tears in my eyes, and I realized that I was as guilty as some others in the way I could sometimes stereotype others. As I thought about Mary's experiences, I thought of how hard that must have been for her. This woman I had previously thought of as somewhat weak and somewhat of a joke, I suddenly realized was a person of great courage and a tower of strength.

I couldn't help but wonder why Mary didn't write poems and stories about her school experiences. I thought, "this is what people would want to know about," and I realized how much harder Mary must have had it in comparison with my own experience. Mary didn't have the luxury of keeping her difference a secret. She started out with students who were openly hostile to her even before they knew who she was as a person. Often she was not given any chance at all, but she faced this discrimination with a grace that I am not sure I would have possessed.

The lesson I learned from Mary that day made me only more determined to face down the prejudices that I sometimes experienced in the school system. Understanding what she went through was a constant reminder that what I was experiencing was not nearly as severe. I wanted very much to show the dignity and determination that Mary had demonstrated.

GAY TEACHERS

For most of my years at Riverside, I was the only gay teacher at the school. However, towards the end of my time at Riverside, I was joined by a lesbian teacher. This didn't relieve much of the isolation I felt since I didn't know for most of the year that this woman was a lesbian. She was an African-American woman who I had become friendly with when we served on several committees together.

At that time, two professors from Morehouse College had been brought in to conduct workshops with the teachers to overcome our racial divisions. The divisions in the school were so pronounced that black teachers and white teachers often distrusted each other. Some of the white teachers were openly racist and blamed all the problems of the school on the African-American students. At any time during the school day, African-American students could be seen wandering the halls because many of the white teachers were so convinced that black students couldn't learn that they would allow them to leave class whenever they asked for permission. In part because of this, the standardized test scores had begun to fall, and there was a chaotic atmosphere throughout the school day.

Despite all of this, the new teacher, Isabel, was very enthusiastic about being a part of the school community, and she had immediately joined the group working to end the racial tensions at the school. My presence on the committee was evidence to her that I didn't harbor the racist views of some of the white teachers. Her presence on the committee showed me that she was someone who wanted to make the school a better place. When she spoke at our meetings, it didn't take me long to realize that we shared a similar philosophy about education, race, and life in general. As we got to know each other, she would frequently come to my classroom to chat.

One day as she was walking through the hallway my classroom was in, she overheard me reprimanding another student. The student, an African-American male, had called another student a faggot. I had taken him out in the hall, and I told him, "I wouldn't let someone use the n word towards you, and I am not going to allow you to call another student a faggot." He agreed to apologize to the student and promised that he wouldn't do it again. I saw Isabel watching the interaction, but I didn't think much of it.

At the end of the day, Isabel came to my room. She immediately asked me if I was gay, and I told her yes. She said, "I thought so. When I overheard you talking to that kid in the hall, I knew no straight teacher would do that." As we began talking about the incident, she explained that she had never heard a straight teacher correct a homophobic remark. She then went on to tell me that she was a lesbian. She didn't want anyone, even the adults, to know it. She told me that she felt more of a need to hide her sexual orientation because it was so much harder to come out in the African-American community.

I knew that she was telling me the truth, but I was saddened by much of the conversation. I was sad that she felt like she couldn't come out, but I was even sadder that she believed that no straight teacher would chastise a student for homophobic remarks. Isabel's situation was much more difficult than mine. Because she felt that she couldn't tell anyone about her identity as a lesbian, she felt even more isolated than I did. Although all of my teacher friends at that time were straight, they were at least aware that I was gay, and I could talk with them about situations that came up at school. Isabel did not have that luxury.

MARCH ON WASHINGTON

In what turned out to be my last year at Riverside, there was a nationwide call for a March on Washington. This decision to have the march caused great controversy in the LGBTQ community. There had been a march in 1987, and many LGBTQ leaders thought that it was too soon to have another march. There were mixed signs about whether or not our strategies were working, especially when it came to national politics. LGBTQ people had worked hard to see that Bill Clinton was elected president, but as soon as he tried to allow lesbians and gays to serve in the military, a backlash took place. This backlash illustrated clearly that LGBTQ people had a long way to go before reaching acceptance.

Because the president seemed to be backing down on the issue of LGBTQ people serving in the military, Clinton became the first president to meet with LGBTQ community leaders. He made it clear that he wouldn't speak at the march and wouldn't even be in town during it. Just as Clinton's decision to not speak at the march caused controversy, so did the picture taken of Clinton's meeting with the LGBTQ leaders. Billy Hileman, one of the activists, had decided that he would wear a gay pride t-shirt and leather vest for the meeting. There was an outcry on the part of more conservative LGBTQ people who thought that Hileman's attire was embarrassing. This was one small crack in the larger fractures that were taking place as the community decided whether to have the march or not.

For LGBTQ people in Georgia, there were plenty of reasons to march. Sam Nunn, our senator and a Democrat, was pushing back on Clinton's plan to allow lesbians and gays to serve openly in the military. Nunn and others would eventually be successful in forcing Clinton to adopt the compromise position of "Don't Ask, Don't Tell." In addition to Sam Nunn's policies, LGBTQ Georgians had to face the fact that the Bower versus Hardwick decision that upheld the sodomy laws started as a case in Georgia. While LGBTQ people in Georgia were under attack statewide, in the city of Atlanta, LGBTQ people were starting to become a political force. Politicians were now attending gay pride events, and they were regularly making LGBTQ issues a part of their political agenda.

When I decided to go to the March on Washington, it was only partially a political move. Most of my decision to attend was based on social reasons. The march promised to bring together gay men from all around the country, and the opportunity to be around this many gay men was certainly not an everyday opportunity. At this time period, just seeing LGBTQ people in large numbers was in itself affirming. I had gone from not knowing that an LGBTQ community existed to being a part of a vast and growing community that was expanding at an exponential pace.

Seeing other gay men was so affirming in that time period that I seized on every opportunity. The two largest LGBTQ events for me in that time were the yearly Gay Pride March, and the visits my friends and I took on Memorial Day and Labor Day to the gay beach at Pensacola. The visits to the gay beach at Pensacola foreshadowed how things were beginning to change. The Pensacola gay beach had started off with a very small number of LGBTQ people who met each year at a part of the beach chosen for no particular reason and unofficially designated it "the gay beach." As word slowly started to spread, the LGBTQ people visiting grew astronomically. As the event grew, party promoters started to rent buildings in town to host large parties for the LGBTQ visitors. The events grew so fast that the residents of Pensacola grew uncomfortable with the huge numbers of LGBTQ tourists, and some residents there started efforts to discourage LGBTQ people from visiting. Citizens of the city wanted council people to take actions to ban LGBTQ visitors. These efforts to discourage LGBTQ visitors were short-lived when ACT-UP encouraged LGBTQ people to stamp all of their money with a pink triangle and the words "gay money." When the business people saw how much money LGBTQ people were spending on these weekends, they quickly changed their minds. The very next year businesses throughout the city put up rainbow flags and welcomed the LGBTQ community. This small skirmish in Pensacola was a microcosm of what was taking place in Atlanta.

As the number of gay pride marchers grew each year, politicians were realizing that they needed LGBTQ votes. The first Gay Pride I attended in Atlanta had around two thousand people. The next one had five thousand. By 1993, the numbers were approaching 100,000 people. It was becoming evident to the politicians in Atlanta that LGBTQ people were becoming a force in the city.

LGBTQ people were becoming more visible on the national level as well, and march organizers hoped that this second March on Washington would be much larger than the earlier one. For me personally, the March on Washington promised to have more LGBTQ people than any event I had ever attended. It also provided the chance to be a small part of history. My hopes for the event were pretty small. I remember hoping that there would be enough people to make the coverage of this event front page news. I wanted people around the country to see that LGBTQ people did exist. At the time, just being visible was a political statement.

The perfect opportunity for me to take the trip also came about. I had dated a man named Alex Wan. This was years before Alex would become the first gay city councilman in Atlanta. Alex was extremely social, and he and some of his friends had formed a group called Interact. The purpose of the group was to provide gay men with a chance to do things as a group outside of the bar. Bars were the main social venue for lesbians and gays at that time, and some lesbians and gays felt that we needed social venues that didn't have alcohol and drugs as the focus. This group would give gay men the opportunity to attend cultural events, go to movies and see plays together. The Interact club was taking a bus to Washington for the march, and my friend Rich and I decided it would be an affordable chance for us to go. I was a little bit worried about the trip because I knew I would have to take a Monday off work because of the bus trip back. I hoped that the march would make national news, and I thought that the students would hear about the march and realize that was the reason for my absence. I had made up my mind that if they asked, I would tell them the truth.

The hours on the bus ride there were grueling, but they were easily overlooked because the trip seemed like an adventure. To help the time go by on the bus ride, I took a book, *Positively Gay: New Approaches to Gay Life*. After the first couple of hours on the bus, most of the people went to sleep, but I stayed up and read. While the march would turn out to be moving, affirming, and educational, this book was equally important in advancing my feelings of solidarity with the LGBTQ community.

The book was one of my increasing purchases at Oxford Books. Over the years in Atlanta I started to find a trip to the bookstore just as exciting as a night at the bar. The LGBTQ books that I found increased my connection to the LGBTQ community just as much as the new LGBTQ friendships I was forming. Through these readings, I had been drawn into a world of exciting new ideas that I couldn't get from my social connections at the gay bars. The book that I read on the bus ride was exposing me to elements of the LGBTQ world that I had never experienced in my life in the South.

When Rich and I got to Washington with the group, we discovered that for this weekend the city became almost entirely gay. Although the media refused to admit the true crowd size, there were well over a million LGBTQ people in town. The events before and during the march were life changing for me. I experienced some historic events that can never be recreated. I can still remember how moved we were by seeing the entire AIDS quilt unveiled. I can remember vividly the speech by Jesse Jackson. Jackson surprised critics and showed enormous courage by speaking at the march when most of the other nationally known politicians had refused to speak. Jackson's courage was even more moving because it highlighted Clinton's absence. As moving as the march was for me, the most moving moments of the trip came about in unexpected ways and from unsung heroes.

One of these moments happened on the first night we

were in town. There was no point in looking for the gay neighborhood. The entire city became a gay neighborhood. On every sidewalk, we were shoulder to shoulder with other LGBTQ people. After walking around for hours on that first night, several of us picked a restaurant simply because it was the closest one around. As we were waiting on our meal, a woman, eating with her son at the table next to us, asked us if we were there for the march. When we told her we were, she said, "I really support your cause." She went on to say that she hoped the march would set records and told us that she had attended the pro-choice rally that had taken place in the weeks before our march. She spoke of the need for all us on the left to maintain solidarity. The fact that this straight mother was supportive of us was incredibly moving to me. There were very few straight people at that time who openly voiced support.

A similar situation happened on the day of the march. Because the city was so crowded with LGBTQ people, the Interact Club had booked a hotel outside the city. Like many other LGBTQ people who were staying in hotels in the suburbs, we had to take a shuttle bus into the city. On the morning of the march, our entire group, around forty to fifty gay men, was waiting to catch the shuttle bus to the Metro Station. As we waited for the bus, I noticed a woman with her child waiting to take the same bus. Most of the gay men I was with didn't even notice the woman, but I started to observe her, and I wondered what was going through the woman's mind when she discovered that the bus would be filled with gay marchers.

When we got on, it was standing room only. I was standing near the woman with the child. The little boy looked up at his mom and said, "Why are all these men holding hands?" His mother stooped down to him, and quietly said, "You know how your daddy and I hold hands because we love each other?" He nodded yes. "Well, these men love each other like your daddy and I do."

This was 1993, and I had never heard anyone address this issue in such a beautiful and straightforward way. As we rode the bus home, I kept thinking about the woman and her explanation. I realized that the march was an important political statement, but it was going to be people like the two mothers I encountered who would really make the changes that we wanted to see take place.

The bus ride back was even more grueling since we didn't have the excitement of the march to look forward to. We took our journey southward away from the freedom of the march environment and back through the conservative communities of the South. When we stopped for breakfast on our way back, I made sure I bought a newspaper before I got on the bus. I just knew that with this many people and such an important event it would be front page news in every major paper. It wasn't. I should have realized that newspapers in the South weren't going to give a great deal of coverage to this event. There was a small article in the paper that I bought, and the media and the National Park Service dramatically undercounted the number of people involved.

When I got back to school, none of the kids had even heard of the march, and so to my surprise there was no explanation needed. No one even asked about it.

DRYDEN HIGH SCHOOL

Even before I went to the March on Washington, I had become more visible in the fight for LGBTQ rights, both in writing and through protests and marches. I worried about how this more visible presence would conflict with my teaching career. I was willing to accelerate my participation in LGBTQ causes because my attendance at the March showed me that silence was no longer an option. My first boyfriend in Atlanta, Mark Conklin, had died of complications due to AIDS while still in his twenties. There were numerous gay bashings in Atlanta at the time, and many of my LGBTQ friends were ruining their lives with excessive drug and alcohol use because of their feelings of being ostracized by the larger society. At that time, I felt that our lives were being threatened, and my career didn't seem very important in comparison. Although not large in number, there were people in the school system who were beginning to notice my activist endeavors.

That I was able to get the job at Dryden despite the reputation I was getting in the school system was due to the support of June. June had left Riverside the year before in order to become the department chair at Dryden. When an opening became available in the English department, she urged me to apply. At the time, I was unsure if I wanted to leave Riverside because it is always a little difficult to abandon the familiar, but June knew that I needed to get a job somewhere that would be more accepting of a gay teacher, and she felt that Dryden would be a better fit. When I was debating whether or not I should leave, I spoke to my friend, Jill, another English teacher. Jill thought I was crazy.

"After the way they have treated you here, you should jump at the chance to go somewhere else," she said.

June made a strong case for my move to Dryden when she told me how many lesbian and gay teachers worked there. At that time, there were at least ten lesbian or gay people on staff, and some of them were even in the administration. June insisted that the gay people on staff were very open and that I would be more comfortable there with other lesbian and gay men as colleagues.

During the interview, I didn't have any worries that Robert Robertson, the principal, would be homophobic. It was clear from the sheer numbers of lesbians and gay men on the faculty that he didn't harbor any fear of hiring an LGBTQ person. In fact, his most trusted assistant principal was a lesbian. Mr. Robertson asked me the standard questions that might be asked during the interview of a potential English teacher. June had prepared me for these questions well in advance, and I thought that I answered them in ways he would approve of. At the end of the interview, he asked me if there was anything else I wanted to add. I briefly thought of saying that I was gay, but I decided against it. I reasoned that straight teachers didn't have to declare that they were straight, so why should I declare that I was gay? Afterwards, I would regret that decision.

I accepted the job, and I quickly saw that the lesbian and gay teachers were not nearly as open as I had thought they would be. None of them were out to the students, and the subject was even taboo among the adults. Undoubtedly, many of the students knew that these teachers were lesbian or gay, but it was never openly discussed by the faculty or with the students. Among the faculty members, everyone knew of the sexuality of the lesbian and gay teachers and even in some cases knew their partners, some of whom taught at other schools or were in administration jobs throughout the county. However, if I ever alluded to the sexuality of any of these people, for example mentioning the person's partner, many of the other teachers would act as if they didn't know what I was talking about. The topic was treated as if everyone understood that these facts shouldn't be discussed.

I had hoped that I would be able to be an openly gay teacher at Dryden, but I found that this was much more myth than reality. During my entire teaching career in Georgia, I never met an LGBTQ teacher who was truly free to be open about her or his identity. Such a person might have existed, but I was not aware of anyone with this freedom. Atlanta Public Schools did add sexual orientation to its non-discrimination policy in the nineties, and the City Schools of Decatur became well-known for its liberal policies and its acceptance of both LGBTQ students and teachers. However, as an employee of my school system, for my entire career I worked with the knowledge that at any time I could be fired simply for being gay, and even in the Atlanta and Decatur schools, I never knew a teacher who was out to the students at that time.

AIDS PLAY

Although the lesbian and gay teachers at Dryden were not completely out, Dryden did provide me with much greater freedom than I had experienced at Riverside. The presence of the lesbian and gay teachers at the school had in their own way made the school culture more accepting for LGBTQ teachers. In addition to that fact, I had June's steadfast support.

The most talked about issue in the LGBTQ community at that time was AIDS. Almost all people who were active in the LGBTQ community knew someone, often many people, who had died. Each week when I picked up a *Southern Voice* or *Etc.* magazine I dreaded looking at the obituary section. I was almost certain to recognize someone I had known at least on a casual basis. Throughout the decade of the eighties, nationwide LGBTQ activists had fought unsuccessfully to get Reagan to even say the word AIDS. George H. Bush continued Reagan's stance and had for the most part ignored the issue. Despite the fact that both Republican presidents had a policy of ignoring the issue, more people in society at large were becoming aware of and concerned about the crisis. Because it was very possible to work on ending AIDS without openly declaring oneself as LGBTQ, mainstream LGBTQ activists used AIDS to focus attention on the gay man as victim angle.

Just as all national issues eventually do, this national awareness surrounding the AIDS crisis was surfacing in schools as well. There were discussions, both nationwide and on a local level, surrounding whether or not high school counseling departments should make condoms available for distribution. Those on the conservative side of the issue were demanding that schools only be allowed to teach abstinence. The issue would surface from time to time in the classroom, and teachers were becoming confused as to what they could and couldn't say to students. Although many objected to any discussion about safe-sex, almost everyone began to agree that it was acceptable to discuss the death toll the disease had taken. LGBTQ activists and their allies wanted this death toll to be discussed in order to end the disease; conservatives wanted the death toll to be discussed as a cautionary tale in order to scare young people away from sex. The stigma associated with those working to end the disease had faded to the point that the participants in the AIDS Walk in Atlanta had moved from being almost exclusively LGBTQ to an almost equal balance of LGBTQ and straight.

The year before I came to Dryden the lesbian and gay teachers on the faculty had already begun to organize groups of students to collect money and to participate in the walk. During my first year at the school, the organizers took it a step further. Prior to the walk, the school performed an AIDS Awareness play. This play was due to the efforts of three teachers. Ford was in charge of handling the production of the play; his friend Michael, the official drama director, helped Ford get the play staged and made arrangements for students to see the production during the school day. Janice, a very popular lesbian teacher, was responsible for the tradition of the AIDS walk itself. In addition to raising money for the walk, the students who chose to participate that first year also tried to raise awareness about the disease throughout the school community by distributing information about how the disease could be spread. The next year, these three teachers had decided a play would reach more of the students and would better raise awareness.

Even though it was my first year at Dryden, all three

of these teachers were well-known to me as larger than life characters in the school community. Being a lesbian or gay teacher at that time required certain strategies developed either consciously or subconsciously. These strategies often resulted in creating an eccentric persona. Luckily, in that time period, eccentricities were often accepted in the school system. In my opinion, all three of the teachers involved had his or her own unique way of navigating being a gay or lesbian teacher. Janice made herself invaluable to the school community by being one of the hardest working teachers in the school. Michael was the jokester who students could always rely on to entertain them, and Ford was one of the most caring teachers in the entire school, so much so that many students called him Uncle Ford.

These three teachers were probably the only three teachers around who could have pulled off the AIDS awareness week and the walk. They were deeply loved by their students, and the students were prepared to do things for these three that they would not have done for other teachers. The play of course took hours of rehearsal, and the walk required students to give up their personal time including the time they spent raising money and an entire weekend afternoon for the walk itself.

After getting the first group of students to walk the previous year, Janice had organized a much larger group of students who pledged to walk and raise money. Ford worked much more actively the second year as well, and besides producing the play, he also took a much larger role in organizing the events that focused on the awareness-raising aspect of the week. On the week leading up to the walk, Ford made a special morning announcement each day. He would read a brief fact about AIDS and express the need for students to take action to end the disease. The students Janice had organized took donations during lunch time. The week ended with the presentation of the play on Friday. To ensure that all the students in the school could see the play, students attended during the one class that all students were required to take, their English class.

I had mixed feelings about all of this. Although I was more active and "out" in the gay community than any of these other teachers, I was a little uncomfortable, especially in my first year at the school, about bringing up a topic that would so clearly cause students to question my identity. My own steps at being more open in the classroom had been tentative at best. The other teachers had established reputations with their students and with the community. I, being new to the school, was still an unknown and untrusted figure.

When the day for the play took place, I had mixed feelings of a different nature. I was astounded that this play was produced on the high school level. One reason for this amazement was the sheer quality of the show. Everything Ford and Michael ever produced at Dryden was good enough to be in any of the professional theaters in Atlanta. Another reason for my amazement was the reaction the play produced on the part of the students. Students really were discussing the play throughout the day, and they were talking about the ways of avoiding contracting or spreading the disease. The students were clearly moved by the production. Some of them were so moved that they convinced other teachers to take them to the production, so many of the students saw the play multiple times.

Of course, being a one-act play, there was not a lot of time for character development, and virtually all of the representations of the groups that might be likely to contract AIDS were stock characters. Coming from my experiences as a teacher at Riverside, I could at times be surprised by the lack of any multicultural sensibility at Dryden. I had noticed the lack of diversity in the school from the very moment I first visited. On the day of my interview at the school, I arrived far too early. While waiting for my appointment, I spent time looking through the yearbook that someone had placed on the coffee table in the lobby. I started counting the number of pages that would go by without having a student of color. With this lack of diversity among the student population, it was no wonder that teachers were often unaware of the stereotypes they were often reinforcing. Watching the play, I was disappointed by the number of stereotypes the production propagated. Although Ford was the director, the influence of Michael was clear in the way the actors played their characters. Because Michael loved to shock, any time there was a gay character in a play at Dryden the gay character was portrayed as very effeminate and an over-the-top stereotype. The gay character in the AIDS play was the quintessential stereotype of what these students might think of when they thought about a gay man. Limp-wristed and mincing, if memory serves me correctly, the actor even played the part with a lisp. This stereotyped portrayal of the gay character wasn't unique to just that character. All the characters were gross stereotypes. For example, the character who got AIDS from drug use was Latino, complete with thick accent and overblown machismo.

To bring up these criticisms to the three teachers in charge seemed unjust to me. Adding to the fact that I had only been at the school for four months was the truth that this play had generated a great deal of discussion and awareness, as was intended. Ford was extremely moved by what he had done, and in most ways with very good reason. Immediately following the play, many of the actors cried because they were so moved by what they had achieved. Years after the play was performed, Ford received letters from students telling him how the play had changed their lives with regard to their attitude towards people with AIDS and with lesbian and gay people in general. Given the emotions surrounding this event, I felt that it would be wrong to protest against the problematic elements of the play.

ISABELLE

That first year at Dryden one of the students I had in class left a lasting impact on me. Isabelle came into the class with a defiant arms-crossed hostility. She had a short boyish haircut and wore mostly jeans and flannel shirts. Even on the first day, I thought, "Wow, what is this kid's problem?" The hostility I sensed was a passive sort of hostility common among certain students. Isabelle never would have tried to disrupt the class. Her hostility was more of the "I dare you to teach me anything" type.

The first breakthrough with Isabelle came from an idea that I had stolen from June. For years, starting when I was at Oak Grove High, I had introduced each class by talking about something in the news for that day. Like

June, I wanted to make the students more aware of what was going on in the world and get them to realize that there were things they could read that would catch their attention.

One of the articles the year I taught Isabelle questioned the wisdom of the Augusta National Golf Club's refusal to admit women as members. This was 1993, and a group of women had started protesting outside the golf course in order to bring attention to the issue. During the comments about this article, Isabelle spoke up without being called on for the first time ever. This breakthrough led to Isabelle speaking with me more both before and after class. The class was British Literature, and Isabelle started bringing me the lyrics to songs by the Indigo Girls with allusions to the literature we were reading in class.

Isabelle's love of the Indigo Girls was somewhat of a clue that she might be lesbian, but it was ambiguous at best. Although the Indigo Girls did have a huge lesbian and gay following, at this time they were at the height of their popularity, and they had more straight fans than gay. Isabelle was so excited by the allusions she had found to the material we had been studying in class that she spent hours making a cassette tape with all the songs that contained these allusions and presented me with it at the end of class one day.

I became more clear about Isabelle's identity when we had a discussion about one of my t-shirts. At the time, I had a Casual Friday tradition of wearing t-shirts throughout February featuring something relating to Black History Month and throughout March something related to Women's History Month. These shirts often caused a great deal of discussion in class. I had to stop wearing one of the shirts because of the confusion it caused. I had a shirt that said, "Feminism is the radical belief that women are people too." Many of the kids didn't get the irony of the slogan and thought I was trying to disparage feminism. The explanation of the real meaning of the shirt took a great deal of time. Being new to the school, I didn't want there to be any chance that students might interpret the shirt in a way I hadn't intended. While it may seem as if the shirt's slogan was impossible to misinterpret, this was all going on at the same time Rush Limbaugh was speaking out every day against "feminazis" and so there was a great deal of hostility directed towards feminists.

Because of the difficulties with the feminism t-shirt, I substituted one that said, "Women constitute half the world's population, perform nearly two-thirds of its work hours, receive one-tenth of the world's income and own less than one-hundredth of the world's property." This shirt caused a certain amount of discussion and explanation also. Someone asked if I was a feminist, and I began an answer that I would give over and over again throughout the years. I said, "Of course I am a feminist. Every male should be a feminist." One of the male students asked why this was the case. I went on to explain, "Many of the males in this class might have sisters. Some of the males in this class will one day marry a woman. Some of the males in this class may one day have daughters. All of the males in the class have a mother. And because you love these women in your life, I am sure you will want them to be treated fairly. That's what feminism is, and that's why every male should be a feminist."

After this discussion about the meaning of the word

feminist, one of the students asked me where I got the shirt, and I replied, "Charis." When the students asked what Charis was, I explained that it was a feminist bookstore in Atlanta. Isabelle came up after the class was over and told me that she was surprised that I knew about Charis, and she then told me that it was her favorite bookstore. I was starting to think Isabelle was a lesbian, but I didn't want to assume anything because I didn't want to be guilty of stereotyping Isabelle simply because she was one of the only teenage girls at that time who identified as a feminist.

The shirt that really got Isabelle's attention was the one I had that depicted Gertrude Stein. We were in the media center that week, and I was walking around checking students' work. As I passed by one of the tables, someone asked me about the shirt. When I told the student that it was a picture of Gertrude Stein, he said, "That is a woman on your shirt?" When I answered yes, he said, "She looks like a man." I replied, "Well, she and her partner at times wore clothing that was traditional for a man." The student asked why, and I responded that I guessed it was because they felt that the clothes women wore during the time period were oppressive. He didn't even think about the fact that I had said the words "her partner," and after repeating, "Well, she looks like a man," and then laughing, he went back to work.

Isabelle was sitting at a table nearby, and she overheard the conversation. She started to ask me questions about Gertrude Stein. When she discovered that Stein was a lesbian, she then proceeded to check out some of the biographies about Stein. I was reminded of my own discovery of Oscar Wilde's homosexuality when I was in high school. After reading these biographies, Isabelle asked me if I could give her some books about gay issues. I started loaning her some of my books. The one that made the biggest impression on her was *Why Can't Sharon Kowalski Come Home?* This book still remains in mind as one of the most moving books I have ever read. The non-fiction work is about the life of Karen Thompson whose partner was injured and became comatose. The book deals with the way Thompson was treated by the parents of her partner, the hospital staff, and the legal community. Thompson and Julie Andrzejewski wrote the book to chronicle the fight to make Thompson the legal guardian of Sharon. Isabelle was as moved as I was by it, and she asked if she could loan the book to a friend. I told her yes, and I soon came to the conclusion that this other young woman and Isabelle were a couple. They both began going to the Emory University library on weekends and started doing research on what had taken place after the book had been published. This was not an easy task since the writers of this work were not well known and there was no internet.

After that year was over and Isabelle's senior year began, I continued loaning more and more books to her. One of the books was Stonewall. Towards the end of the year, when it was time to do her research paper for her senior English class, Isabelle came to me and told me that she wanted to do Stonewall as her research paper but that she was afraid to announce it as her topic when the students had to say out loud what their topic would be. She was also worried that she might be asked about her topic in front of other students as the research process went on. Her teacher was Sally Eliot, and we had become friends during that first year. I could tell right away that Sally wasn't homophobic, so I assured Isabelle that it would be alright and that I would talk to Mrs. Eliot about it.

When I spoke to Sally about Isabelle's idea, she was very receptive to Isabelle's topic. Sally assured me that she wouldn't ask Isabelle any questions about her topic when other students might overhear. Up to this point, I hadn't thought before about the pressure that teachers, like myself, unknowingly put on students. Sally's usual method, like my own, was to have students call out the topic they were planning to work on. By having the students call it out, we could ensure that no one had the same topic and expose students to the wide range of possibilities for research. In the past, Sally had also asked students to discuss problems that they were encountering with their topic. By doing this, other students could offer struggling students suggestions. With Isabelle in mind, Sally had to alter the way she taught the research paper. That year she made sure that students didn't have to tell other students what they were working on. She made the reporting of preliminary results voluntary rather than required. Luckily for me, Sally was very sensitive to Isabelle's needs and the research project went on without any problems. But it was a reminder to me of the many ways LGBTQ students were being silenced without teachers even realizing it.

NATIONAL FACULTY

At the end of my first year at Dryden, 1994, I had an experience that would change my entire career as an educator. While I was still teaching at Riverside, June chose me to participate in a program that the school system was offering in conjunction with The Smithsonian. Michael Lomax, at the time the chairman of the Board of Commissioners, was dedicated to the arts, and he was instrumental in bringing the program to the schools. The Smithsonian ultimately included five metro areas in the program. The program was called The National Faculty, and it was designed to give teachers an intellectual outlet on a higher level. This program involved a partnership between public school teachers and university scholars. Elementary, middle and high school teachers would attend seminars conducted by the scholars, and as the program went on, a dialogue between university professors and public school teachers would ensue. Monthly meetings would be held at museums located in the metropolitan area of each region. This would give teachers greater knowledge of and access to the resources these museums offered for educational purposes.

Each summer, six teachers in each of the regional groups would be chosen by lottery to go to Washington, D.C. and have an extended seminar that would familiarize the participants with the programs the Smithsonian offered. The second summer, I was one of the winners of the lottery.

I was nervous about the trip because we were staying in dorms at American University. This brought up my fears from my childhood and teenage years about being in close proximity to heterosexual males. There were an odd number of males in the Atlanta group, and this meant I would be rooming with someone I didn't know. I didn't know how this man was going to take the idea of finding out that he had a gay roommate. When I got there and discovered that my roommate was a retired military man, I was even more concerned about it. But I must say the man handled the situation well. Maybe it was his years in the military that prepared him for sharing a room with different types of people, but he was one of the most accepting of all the members of the group.

The Atlanta group arrived early to American University, where we would be staying. We were provided with meal passes and metro passes. Since we were staying at the university, getting into the city required taking a shuttle bus to the metro station, and then taking the metro into town.

The first afternoon of the trip we were on our own since all the members hadn't arrived yet. One of the members of the Atlanta group, Nancy, decided that since I was going into town, she wanted to go with me. When I told her that I was going to walk around the gay area of the city, she didn't hesitate and went right along. In the late eighties and throughout the nineties, one of the best aspects of visiting a different city was this exploration of the "gayborhoods." Walking around the Dupont Circle area of Washington was as exciting for Nancy as it was for me. I had been to D.C. during the march, but with the city that crowded, I hadn't really had an opportunity to explore.

Because there was no internet at the time, and information was much harder to come by, I made use of my copy of *The Damron's Guide*. Using this book, Nancy and I were able to identify and visit the gay bookstores and bars and coffeehouses. Nancy and I quickly became friends, which was a good thing since many others in the group would turn out to be far less accepting of a gay man's participation in the group.

By the next day everyone had arrived, and all thirty-three of us, six people from each of the five regions and the three professors, boarded the bus for a tour of the city. Because of my experiences with watching so many die of AIDS, I was becoming more and more open about being gay. I came out to a few members from Seattle right away. We were seated next to each other on the bus, and they had seen me running earlier in the morning. They asked me if I had been in the military. When I looked puzzled, they explained that they thought I might have been because of the run and because of my short haircut, and I responded, "No. This is just the standard gay boy haircut where I am from." There was a bit of shocked looks on their faces, but they were very polite about it.

When we got to the seminar on that first day, we had to go around the circle and state what kind of project we wanted to work on for the month. All the people in the group told very personal stories about how they chose the project they wanted to work on.

When my turn came, I said, "We always hear that the personal is political, and listening to all of you tell your stories, it seems that it is academic also. I would like to do my project on gay and lesbian issues especially as they concern students. I recently watched a 20/20 episode documenting the Harvey Milk School in New York. It is a school for gay kids that don't get along in traditional schools. During the show, one young woman in describing her public school experience said, 'When they called me nigger, everyone said you can't do that, but when they called me dyke, no one said anything.' I want to work on what we could do to better address the needs of these kids." A silence fell over the group.

During the break, one of the scholars who was leading the group, Kimberly Phillips, came over and started a discussion with me. She commented on a t-shirt I was wearing and asked me if it referred to a gay topic. She immediately started talking about her feelings about LGBTQ rights and offered her support for my project. Kimberly was an African-American scholar who had done her dissertation work on The Great Migration. I immediately felt a bond with her that continued through-out the program.

One of the first assignments we had as a group was to present our city to the other members. We were given no real guidelines, and so it was left to us as to how this would be done. When the Atlanta group met, we started to give suggestions. An older woman in the group said that she happened to have a slide show with her containing scenes from the history of Georgia and Atlanta. She suggested that we go through the slides for our presentation. I expressed my belief that this would seem like some kind of travel agent's display, and I wanted us to focus on some of the social issues that were prominent at the time.

With that in mind as we prepared our presentation, I thought some discussion of how issues of multiculturalism were playing out on a local and regional level might be in order. I suggested that we might talk about the Georgia flag, which at that time featured the Confederate flag prominently. I said we might discuss the use of the Braves as the mascot of Atlanta's baseball team, and I thought we might talk about Cobb County, Georgia which was in the news at that time because the county commission had just passed an ordinance saying that gays and lesbians were not welcome in their county.

Most of the members of the group were horrified by this suggestion. Why did I want to bring up negative aspects that most people would rather forget? I pointed out that this group was filled with intellectuals and probably would not want a bland tourist's guide to Atlanta. A polite argument ensued as most members of the group felt that my idea was too radical. As the argument about this continued, I pointed out that the other groups were dealing with some of these same issues in their own cities, and they would be unlikely to look down on Atlanta for the same issues they were dealing with in their home cities. I used the Washington Redskins as a prominent example.

An African-American man in the group said that he liked the idea of the social issues, but he wanted to only focus on the flag issue and ignore the others. He felt the idea of racial disparities was a large enough topic to be dealt with on its own. The group ended in disarray. Everyone was arguing with each other. I agreed to drop the entire idea. No one was happy, and so we all agreed to meet later after we had time to think over the ideas.

One of the members of the group was an African-American woman, and she pulled me aside. We had met in her dorm room, and Jerri kept me in the room after the others left. She started talking to me about the oppression she had faced in her life, and said that she could relate to what I was experiencing with this discussion. She felt that her ideas were often ignored because she was an African-American woman. She said that even when working for African-American civil rights her ideas had been ignored by the men in the group. She wanted me to know that she supported me, and she told me that I should ignore the anger expressed by other members of the group. She insisted that we should find a way to include my ideas in the presentation.

Several of the members of our group were still outraged by my suggestion a couple of days later, and I started to think a bigger part of their emotional reaction was due to being a part of the only group that had an openly gay person in it. This thought occurred to me when one of the women in the group told me that she was embarrassed by me. We had taught together at Oak Grove, and she said that she couldn't believe the way I was acting. She pointed out that she had always liked me when I was at Oak Grove. Her main problem with my "behavior" on this trip was the t-shirts I had been wearing.

All through the trip I wore a different political t-shirt each day. This woman told me that people were starting to avoid being near me on the bus because they didn't want to be seen with someone who was so obviously expressing radical ideas. She insisted that she knew that I was a good person, and she questioned why I was acting differently on this trip. When I expressed to her that she had only seen me in my professional life, and that I wasn't acting any differently than I did in Atlanta, it dawned on her that I hadn't gone out and bought a wardrobe of t-shirts for this one trip. I had noticed that other members of the group had avoided being near me on our bus trips from American University to the Mall. Kimberly and the other scholars had noticed this too, and they always made it point to stand near me on these bus rides.

Our presentation of our city was to take place on the first Friday of the trip. As we got closer to the presentation day, we continued to discuss the ideas in an informal way during breaks and at lunch. When we met again, Nancy suggested that instead of having one group presentation, everyone in the group should have a certain number of minutes to present his or her own version of Atlanta. The people in the group embraced the idea, and we decided to pick out a certain number of slides as background for our presentation. Nancy decided to focus on Georgia authors, and I used my time to present four social issues that were prominent at the time. I left out the flag issue since the African-American man was using his minutes to deal solely with that issue.

When all the presentations were over, the scholars in the group pointed out that their favorite had been the Atlanta presentation. One of the scholars said that he had worried when it started that this would be a Chamber of Commerce tour of Atlanta, but then he pointed out that the presentation started to take a turn when Nancy used a quote from W. E. B. Du Bois to describe Atlanta, "South of the North and North of the South lies the land of many hills." He then started discussing the social issues that I brought up. Since I had pointed out how the other cities involved were facing many of these same problems, he used that as a basis for the discussion that took place immediately after the presentation. He asked the group how we came up with this idea for our presentation. The woman who had been so angry with me about the t-shirts encouraged me to speak up, but I sat back quietly as the others explained the process we went through in a way that veiled the gay issues that had sparked so much controversy.

At the end of the day, a woman from a different group

came up to me and complimented me on my speaking ability. Then she said, "Several of us were talking about it, and we were glad you brought up those other social issues because if you had just brought up the gay issue, we would have been angry." Clearly, she didn't realize her homophobia, and incidents like this would continue to occur throughout the program.

As the program went on, I began my research for the program, which involved interviewing gay men about their high school experiences. I learned most from my free time spent in the gay neighborhood in Washington. I spent hours at Lambda Rising, the gay bookstore in Dupont Circle. While I was in the store searching the shelves one afternoon, I happened on a book called *Chicana Lesbians: The Girls Our Mothers Warned Us About*. In the program, we had been reading Sandra Cisneros' *The House on Mango Street*, and so when I saw her name on the cover as one of the reviewers, it immediately caught my eye. Our discussion of the book was to take place later in the week. As I read Cisneros' review of the book, her words were so profound I wrote them down in my notebook before leaving the store: "When I was selling books at a Chicana conference, I noticed book browsers were literally afraid to touch this anthology. I say now what I said then, 'Don't be afraid. Sexuality is not contagious, but ignorance is.' If you've ever been curious, been there, been voyeur, been tourist, or are just plain under-informed, misinformed, or unaffirmed, here is a book to listen and learn from."

Later in the week, during our discussion of *The House on Mango Street*, I asked if it might be possible that Cisneros was a lesbian. The people in the group got furious with me. How dare I suggest that this famous author who they all admired might be a lesbian? I pointed out the curious inscription in the book, "I am nobody's mother and nobody's wife." Even one of the scholars who had been very supportive about LGBTQ issues seemed angry that I would ask this. He stated that it was unimportant and said we should move on to other aspects of the novel.

I wasn't surprised by the professor's reaction to my comment. The professors were some of the most supportive people in the group when it came to my topic, but at times their own internalized homophobia would surface. They did try to incorporate topics into the program because of my participation in it. For example, the program frequently provided movies for us to watch at night. Because of my presence in the program, they included a documentary about the making of AIDS Memorial Quilt. When they talked about LGBTQ issues, it was almost always in the context of the AIDS crisis. Perhaps they felt this was a way to bring in LGBTQ issues without giving offense to the rest of the group. While I did appreciate their efforts to include me, it was a reminder that the only thing that people thought of at that time when they thought of LGBTQ people was AIDS or gay people as victims.

Many people in the group didn't make any attempts to hide just how uncomfortable they were with my topic. While several members of the group were getting more comfortable with having a gay man as part of the group, a majority of the people in the group would frequently make subtle remarks to me to let me know that my presence made them personally uncomfortable. Sometimes on the weekends we would all go to a bar together. One night when someone suggested it might be fun to go to a gay bar, the rest of the group reacted with horror.

By the time that we got to our final presentation, I had become fed up with the attitudes of most of the members. Nancy had drawn the first spot when we decided the order of presentations, but I talked her into letting me have the spot. Rather than give an overview of the research I had done or the interviews I had conducted, I gave this speech:

First, I want to explain why I wanted to go first today. The reason I decided to go first is last week a few of you kind of pulled me aside at lunch or during break to ask me questions about my life as a gay man. I wanted to let you know that I am open to that, and that it is ok to ask questions. I am pretty widely read in lesbian and gay studies, so I probably will be able to answer your questions. If I can't, I probably can tell you where to find the answers. But I have to let you know that I am not the representative of all of gay and lesbian America. I think I am giving some of you the wrong idea because last week people I talked to said, "I don't know any lesbians or gays." The first thing I want to clear up is that idea. All of us know many lesbian and gay people. Every survey that has ever been done, except one, shows that gay people make up somewhere around ten percent of the population. Imagine, one in ten people is lesbian or gay. What this means in your classroom is that in a class of thirty, obviously three people are gay or lesbian. Start multiplying that number, three, times the number of classes you have taught, and you will see that you know many gays and lesbians.

Kim told us on the first day, "We all need to be burdened by each other's history." She repeated it yesterday just in case you didn't get it the first time. But this presents me with a problem because how do I bring the history of these people to you when the latest survey shows that sixty-five percent of the American population is tired of hearing about gay rights. In the course of doing my project, the entire project had to be changed because of this fact. I started thinking, "How do I do this?" At first I thought I could bring you the story of William Metz, who was stabbed to death by a skinhead. I could bring you the story of Amekaeyla Gaston, who was run over by two men on her way to the Michigan Womyn's Festival. She was run over by two men who had been drinking all day and had said they wanted to go have some fun with the lesbians.

But I decided this is too easy. When we hear these stories, we say, "Well, I'm not part of this. I haven't killed anybody or beaten anybody up." But I started to realize it's not the people who stand on the side of the road with their, "Thank God for AIDS" signs that hurt my community. It's the things people do every day. I want to give you a few examples to illustrate my point.

The first one is from Saturday night. When I went into the community room, several of you were trying to decide where to go dancing. Molly suggested everybody should go to Tracks, a gay bar. I wish I had a camera to capture your expressions. I would like to be able to play it back now and let you see your expressions and hear your comments. What I would like you to do now is imagine. What I want you to imagine is me coming and getting each of you individually rather than as a group, taking you to a gay bar, and locking you in there for seven days a week, twenty-four hours a day. When you are able to imagine that, you will know what lesbians and gays feel like in your world every day.

The next example is from the day we went to see the Thomas Cole exhibit. I was wearing this shirt [two sailors kissing with the caption "Read My Lips" underneath]. I started to leave with my bookbag in hand. Two people walked out in front of me with their bags. When I started to walk out, the guard told me to stop and said he would have to check my bag. The entire time he was checking it, he kept saying, "I want you to know this is not because of who you are. This is not because of who you are."

A couple of you told me that you were offended by this shirt because it shows two men kissing. I have to tell you that the other day when we were over at Arlington National Cemetery, I was not thinking what all of you were thinking. What I was thinking was, "We are over here working ourselves into some kind of patriotic frenzy over these men who kill other men. We go to movies and somehow manage to enjoy watching men commit the most gruesome acts of violence against each other, and somehow that is ok. But the thought of two men making love to each other...well there is no way we can accept that. That is going too far."

Now these things don't hurt me that much because I am a grown man. But what I am worried about is what happens to the children. Last year the federal government did a study that showed while lesbians and gay men make up only ten percent of the population, they make up thirty-three percent of all teenage suicides. I realized what an impossible problem this would be to overcome when I told my friend Sophie this fact. I told her someday a kid is going to come to you and say, "I want to kill myself because I'm gay or I'm a lesbian." Sophie told me, "I will have to tell that kid I can't help you because I don't believe in who you are or what you do." Now, when we have people who would rather see a child kill him or herself rather than accept the fact that the child is lesbian or gay, we have some serious problems.

I just want to make one other point. The other day I raised the issue of whether or not Cisneros was a lesbian. At first, there was anger that I would even suggest such a thing. Then, there was the attitude that it doesn't make any difference because she is writing about the heterosexual experience. I want to tell you that it does matter for two reasons. Number one, it matters because we need to break this code of silence. Number two, it matters because if Cisneros is a lesbian, and I am not saying she is, but if she is, it makes the reading of that book a very different text. Oscar Wilde wrote about the heterosexual experience also. But he wrote about that culture not as a participant in it, but as an observer of it. And that makes the reading of his work a very different thing.

I want to finish off with a quote from Cisneros. This is from a book Cisneros was reviewing called Chicana Lesbians: The Girls Your Mother Warned You About. *"When I was selling books at a Chicana conference, I noticed book browsers were literally afraid to touch this anthology. I say now what I said then, 'Don't be afraid. Sexuality is not contagious, but ignorance is.' If you've ever been curious, been there, been voyeur, been tourist, or are just plain under-informed, misinformed, or unaffirmed, here is a book to listen and learn from." Finally, I just want to urge all of you to read something about gay and lesbian teenagers or gays and lesbians in general because that is what you would do for any other type of child you teach.*

After I gave the speech, I returned to my seat. The group had applauded loudly for me, and I could see that I definitely had the support of the scholars with what I had said. Nancy got up and gave her presentation saying that she didn't really want to follow me. During her presentation, I tried to make constant eye contact with her because I realized that everyone in the group had his or her gaze focused on me. After Nancy's presentation, the scholars decided that we should take a break, even though only two of us had presented. I could not even make it to the restroom because so many people wanted to comment about what I had said. Over and over, they said they hadn't noticed that their actions and comments had been homophobic. Many of them wanted to tell me how great the quote was by Cisneros. One of them even went so far as to say, "I think you could really change that quote and put a lot of things in there other than the word sexuality." The fact that she was eager to change the quote made me think that she was subconsciously still harboring a great deal of homophobia.

That afternoon while I was in my dorm room, one of the members of the group knocked on the door and asked if she could talk with me. As soon as she came in, she proceeded to tell me that she was a lesbian. I had not even suspected that she might be, and she talked for an hour about how much she wanted to come out but just couldn't do it. She was well liked by the members of the group from her hometown, but not a single one of them knew that she was lesbian. She felt that because she was a teacher, she couldn't reveal her true identity to any of her friends. It reminded me of the fact that those of us who had the ability to speak out had to do it because for every one of us who could speak out, there were thousands who didn't have that luxury.

I left the National Faculty program with the clear understanding that I had not been one of their favorite participants. My insistence on bringing up LGBTQ issues had introduced an element they had not been prepared for. Nevertheless, in many ways, the program worked for me in just the way the Smithsonian had intended. The program was supposed to inspire public school teachers to become interested in higher levels of research, and I came back from the program determined to go back to school. My exposure to Kimberly Phillips made me aware of something I hadn't previously considered. I realized that Kimberly had gotten her Ph.D. by focusing on a very specific area of interest to her, the Great Migration of African-Americans from the South to the North. I realized that I had not done as well as I might have in undergraduate school or when working towards my master's degree because I hadn't been completely interested in the topics I was studying. I decided I would pursue a specialist's degree, and this time I would make every assignment have something to do with LGBTQ issues. I was no longer worried that it wouldn't work. The National Faculty program had helped me discover that there was a place for LGBTQ studies in academia.

AIDS AWARENESS WEEK REDUX

When school started back in the fall, Janice asked me to help out with AIDS Awareness Week. We began planning immediately. Ford was intending to continue with the morning announcements as he had done in the past, and Janice was planning to organize the students for the walk once again. Ford didn't feel that he could recreate the play since most of the students had seen it the previous year. I had suggested that we ask English teachers to read a story about someone with AIDS. I had chosen a chapter from Anthony Godby Johnson's *A Rock and a Hard Place*. The book is the true story of an adolescent who had contracted AIDS and the struggles he faced.

A couple of weeks before these events were to take place, the principal called Janice in to tell her that AIDS Awareness Week had been canceled. He explained that a couple of parents had voiced opposition to the events that would go on during the week. Their reasons, Janice was told, were twofold. They said that they felt the students were too young to be exposed to the idea of gay people, and they claimed that some students had gone without lunch in order to donate their lunch money the previous year. Janice was stunned. She wondered why in an area that was as affluent as the Dryden school district these parents wouldn't consider it a great thing to see their children do without every once in a while to help those less fortunate.

June immediately stepped in to try to help. She got one of the assistant principals, Lily, to go in to see Mr. Robertson with her. Lily was a closeted lesbian who was very well-respected by Mr. Robertson. After the meeting,

Mr. Robertson was still adamant that the week would not take place. However, June assured me that she thought she would be able to change his mind over time.

Although I respected June immensely, I didn't agree with her. I knew that Mr. Robertson, as good a man as he was, would not go against these parents. One of the things I discovered about the school system is that parents have all the power. As a teacher I could complain or could point out different and better ways to do something, and I would be completely ignored. But if a single parent complained, the administration would move with the utmost speed to placate the parent.

Janice was distraught that the week was called off. I was angry. That afternoon, while I was at the gym with my friend Anthony, I told him what had happened. As we talked, Anthony and I started to form a plan. Having been arrested while fighting to prevent AIDS, Anthony was one of ACT-UP Atlanta's most prominent members. Anthony and I both anonymously called the ACT-UP hotline and left messages that would lead people to believe that we were the parents of students at Dryden. We didn't lie, but we certainly gave a different impression than the truth. We wanted it to seem as if this was coming from people in the Dryden community, rather than outsiders. We said how upset we were that the principal had canceled the week, and that we felt that children needed to hear and become educated about the disease.

The next day, Mona Love, one of the most outspoken of the ACT-UP activists called the school. Mrs. Ford, the secretary, was a white woman in her sixties. When she received the call and the woman identified herself as someone from the AIDS Coalition to Unleash Power calling regarding the canceled AIDS Awareness Week, Mrs. Ford almost went into shock. However, she would not let Mona talk to Mr. Robertson. Mrs. Ford wanted to give Mr. Robertson time to think about how he should respond to this radical group.

Mr. Robertson must have called Lily into his office because halfway through the day, Lily called me in for a talk. She asked if I knew anything about the incident. I said that my workout partner was a member of ACT-UP and that he had mentioned to me that he knew about some calls to the hotline. Lily asked me what ACT-UP intended to do. It became clear to me that Mr. Robertson had decided that the lesbian administrator would provide the best means of getting the gay teacher to reveal what he knew. I quickly decided to use this strategy to my advantage. I said, "Well, Anthony told me that if the school wasn't going to have AIDS Awareness Week, ACT-UP would bring AIDS Awareness to them."

"Randy, what do you mean by that?"

"Anthony said they would come to the homecoming game and pass out condoms."

"Randy, it would be illegal for them to come on campus."

"They won't come on campus. They will stand on the sidewalk outside the football stadium and pass out condoms. I want you to know that if it comes to that, I will feel compelled to help them. The local news stations will probably want to film me since I will be a teacher participating in the protest. This will probably be a big local news story."

My experience had taught me that there is only one thing that the school system fears more than parents, and that is news coverage. I am sure that when Lily told Mr. Robertson what I had said, they both conjured up visions of an unkempt looking group of people in leather passing out condoms to high school students on their way to the game. One thing my experience during the race riots at Riverside had taught me was that a scene such as the one I was getting them to imagine couldn't help but bring in the local news programs. I didn't worry that I was making this plan up on the spot because I knew that the members of ACT-UP would love nothing more than to carry it out.

June and I got into one of the few arguments we ever had over the issue:

"Randy, I don't understand why you just couldn't wait for me to handle it. I would have talked to Mr. Robertson, and I would have brought him around."

"No, I don't think you would have."

"We'll never know that because you didn't give me the chance."

"June, many of these straight men might disagree with you about feminism, but they realize that they can't do without women. When they disagree with me as a gay man, they react with the knowledge that they would be only too glad to do without gay men. I was going to do whatever it took to show them that we weren't going to be pushed around."

The next day I gave June a card with a quote from Rumi, "Out beyond ideas of right and wrong, there is a field. I'll meet you there."

Two days after my meeting with Lily, Mr. Robertson called everyone involved with the AIDS Awareness Week into the conference room. He told us that he was unsure how we had gotten the idea that the week had been canceled. It had not been canceled, he said. It had merely been put on hold while he tried to address the concerns of the parents. He told us that a committee would be formed to work with us on the various events for the week.

June took charge of the committee, and she made sure to include parents, teachers, and administrators. She went over the plans, and she gave members of the committee the reading I had chosen. Far from being offended, the parents were moved by Anthony Johnson's story. I had deliberately chosen a section that wouldn't reveal how Johnson had contracted the disease. The parents, merely out of curiosity, wanted to know how he had become infected, and I refused to tell them or any of the teachers who would use the story. I pointed out that I didn't want people to think that some people were innocent victims while others got what they deserved.

Janice organized a large group of students to participate in the actual walk. She made t-shirts to help raise money. The t-shirts had a graphic design with the words, "When future generations ask what you did to end the AIDS crisis, what will you say?" Ford prepared announcements to be read throughout the week by different faculty members to show that they were supportive of the cause. The committee unanimously approved all aspects of the plans for the week.

It was clear to me that the parents were more comfortable now that June, a heterosexual woman, was in charge, and I greatly appreciated June's willingness to lead the group, especially after our argument, But the important thing was that the week's events took place. For Janice and Ford, the main concern was that the students would get the information that might someday save their life, but for me, the important thing had changed from the distribution of this information to the need to show the administration that the lesbian and gay teachers were not going to be oppressed.

THE WRITER'S PALETTE

As far as size and scope, one of the most homophobic things I ever witnessed in a school occurred because of a writing contest. Ironically, it was not intentional on anyone's part, but was merely a product of the culture of that time period. The writing contest that spurred this incident was the brainchild of a tremendous teacher, Elizabeth Turner. Elizabeth was quirky and eccentric, and she could get students to go well beyond the required work for her class.

To make sure every child participated in the contest, Elizabeth had decided that each English class should choose one winner from the writings on a particular topic. All of the winners from classes that met during the same period of the day would read their work at an assembly for all the students who had English during that class period. Each class period's presentation would be completely unique since each period would have a different set of winners.

On the day of the assemblies, Elizabeth had decorated the auditorium to look like a coffee house. Elizabeth and some of the students wore berets. Each assembly that first year was a complete success. The students were polite when listening to the readings of the winning pieces, and there was a literary feel to the program that went beyond anything that might be expected in a high school setting.

The success of that first year surprisingly worked against the program for the future years. In the programs during that first year, the pieces that were comical were scarce, but they were of course the most popular ones with the audiences. By the second year of the program students were increasingly going for a comic effect, and by the third year, almost all the students had given up on serious pieces.

It was during the third year of the program that the homophobic incident took place. Students in one teacher's first period class had decided that instead of writing a piece, they wanted to create a video. In that time period, creating a video took a considerable amount of skill on the part of the students, and video presentations were not commonplace, as they are today.

As the movie started during the first period assembly, I had immediate problems with the content. The premise of the movie was based on a nerdy kid who wanted to fit in with the more affluent and popular students. The popular crowd didn't want him, in part because he couldn't afford a Polo shirt. The student playing the part of the nerdy character played it with a very effeminate voice and was clearly meant to be a gay stereotype. As the movie went on, the nerdy character tried to make a plain shirt into a Polo shirt by making a paper Polo symbol and adhering it to his shirt. At first the popular students accepted him as part of the group. As the plot continued, the popular students discovered the fraud and exposed the student by ripping the fake monogram off the shirt. The movie ended with the popular students chasing the nerdy student in order to catch him and beat him up. The students laughed uproariously. I sat through the movie stone faced.

While sitting through the movie, I thought that I would talk to the teacher whose class had created the video and share my concerns. When I returned for the second period assembly, to my surprise, the video was shown again. The same thing happened third period. When I asked Elizabeth why this movie was playing during each class period when it was the winner for first period's class, she told me that the video had been such a hit with the first period that the filmmakers wanted it shown during every assembly. I raised my objections, but during the five minutes between class, I couldn't go into detail on every point. Elizabeth thought I was reading too much into the movie. The movie was played in every class period during that day, and that meant that by the end of the day, everyone in the school had seen it.

During my lunch time, I started writing a letter to the principal explaining in detail why I thought it was reprehensible. I started out with the classism expressed in the movie through the student's exclusion based on not being able to afford a Polo shirt. I then moved on to the sexism and homophobia based on the gross stereotypes in the characterization used in the movie. I ended by pointing out the fact that besides encouraging students to laugh at gay people, the movie inadvertently supported gay bashing. I showed the letter to my friend and fellow English teacher, Clare. Not only did Clare agree with the points I brought out, she asked me if she could join me in signing the letter. We signed, and I delivered the letter to the principal's office.

At the end of the day, Lily, the assistant principal,

called me to the office. Even though she was a lesbian, she said that she didn't see any of these things until I pointed them out. She said that she was sure that the students were so entertained by the movie that they didn't take time to analyze these deeper points. Rick, the English teacher in whose class the movie was made, was one of the most liberal teachers in the school, but he said until I pointed these things out, he hadn't seen them either. He apologized and told me that he planned to go over the points I had made with the students who made the film.

For me, this film epitomized the culture of that time period. Our society was so saturated with homophobia that even when it was staring us in the face, we couldn't see it.

SPECIALIST DEGREE

As soon as I returned from the National Faculty program, I enrolled in the specialist program at Georgia State. Of course, I would still teach full-time, but I would take classes at night and during the summer for the next two years.

I was determined to follow the plan I had decided on during my time with Kimberly Phillips and focus every assignment on something having to do with LGBTQ people. This was much easier than I had thought it would be. Almost every class had an obvious place where my research would work, and the classes that didn't have an obvious place still provided openings for my topic.

It turned out that my research could be used on a practical level in my high school setting when teachers turned to me for help. Eva, Janice's partner, started this pattern of asking me for help when she asked me to write a letter to a teacher whose class she was taking during her graduate school counseling program. The teacher had expressed some homophobic comments that were based on her Christian religious beliefs. Eva felt that she didn't have enough knowledge of the Bible to refute the teacher's comments, but she also didn't want them to stand without confronting them in some way. I wrote the letter that Eva requested, and I got a response from the professor. However, her response showed that she was steadfast in her original opinion that LGBTQ people were sinful and needed to change their ways.

Shortly after Eva asked me for help, another special education teacher came to me and said she needed my help. She was team teaching with a science teacher who was fairly young. This teacher frequently left his classroom during the class. This was fine in the classes that this woman team taught with him because she could supervise the students in his absence. However, some of the students in his other classes came to her with a concern. These students said that when this teacher left class, students would often start roughhousing and wrestling around with each other. When the teacher would return, he would stop this behavior by saying, "Stop wrestling with each other. What are you a bunch of homosexuals?"

The special ed teacher didn't want to confront him about it because she had to work with him throughout the year. She asked me to talk to him on behalf of the students. I spoke with June, and I told her that I wanted to use some of my research about LGBTQ teen suicides. She cautioned me about this and asked me if I wanted him to stop doing it only out of a sense of guilt. She also warned me that this might make him even more adamant to continue these comments.

I met with the teacher one afternoon as soon as school got out. As soon as we started talking, I saw that he was getting embarrassed, but he also readily admitted that he did frequently make the statement that was reported. I went on and talked to him about the number of LGBTQ kids who committed suicide. I gave him some research I had copied concerning the difficulties LGBTQ teens face. He looked at the research and said, "Well. If I can't say what I have been saying, then I guess I just won't say anything at all. I think that gay people are going to hell, and I don't want to act like I support this in any way."

I replied, "I want to leave this information with you if I can, and you can look over it when you have more time. I appreciate what you are saying, and I don't want to try to force you to change your opinion. I also know that if something I said caused a student to commit suicide, I would regret it for the rest of my life." I left the information with him and realized that I had just done what June had cautioned me about. I felt bad that I was relying on guilt to make this teacher stop his homophobic statements, but I reasoned that the most important thing was to get him to stop before he did real damage.

While the research I was doing at Georgia State was helping me at Dryden, it was also helping me grow as a writer and a person. I had a lack of confidence in my writing ability in part due to my experience in the master's program. However, in the specialist program my research was winning over professors in every class. Tired of reading the same or very similar papers about transactional analysis, reader response theory, and meta-analysis, I think the professors were more than happy to see a paper on something they weren't all that familiar with.

One of the classes during the specialist program that went a long way towards showing me that my voice could be heard was a class taught by Bob Probst. Dr. Probst had a reputation for being very free-spirited in his approach to class. I had several classes with him during my master's program, and I had great respect for his theories about English education. The class I took with him during this specialist program was a writing course, and he told us that we should create our own final assignment by choosing what type of writing we were interested in and what we wanted to write about.

I decided to write letters. My letters were wide ranging and were most often a response to something that was going on in the news. They mostly dealt with LGBTQ issues, but at times they ventured into other areas I was interested in. They almost all dealt with some area of controversy.

One was to the Nike company in praise of their ad featuring Ric Munoz, the first ad to feature an HIV-positive athlete. Conservatives had denounced the ad, and I wanted to be one of the people who showed support for the company. Another letter concentrated on a local issue. In his political race, Mitch Skandalakis, a Fulton County Commissioner, had tried to invoke racism in his bid for reelection by making the picture of his opponent, a black man, appear darker than it actually was. He had also asserted that all HIV-positive athletes should be forced to disclose their status before competing. This was during the time period that Greg Louganis had come out as HIV-positive shortly after competing in the Olympics. Other letters dealt with funding for the National Endowment for the Arts and National Public Radio. Both were under fire because Republicans had deemed them as being too liberal. In another letter, I chastised The Atlanta Journal for its lack of coverage of Republican Congressman Dick Armey's reference to openly gay Congressman Barney Frank as Barney Fag.

My favorite letter during this time period was one I wrote to the Denny's Restaurant Chain. This was 1994, and Denny's was in the midst of charges of racism. The restaurant was accused of refusing service to black customers, making black customers they did seat wait longer than white customers and overcharging black customers when it came time to pay. The company later settled these lawsuits by paying 54 million dollars to the victims. The letter I wrote was in regard to a situation that happened at the Denny's Restaurant that was located in Midtown, Atlanta. A gay couple was dining there, and one of the male partners had his arm on the back of the booth behind his partner's head but not touching his partner in any way. A heterosexual customer complained about this "public display of affection," and the couple was denied service and forced to leave the restaurant.

There were numerous other letters, and as part of the assignment, I had to share them with the class. None of the letters caused any controversy until I wrote one about Alexander the Great. A lengthy article had appeared in *The Atlanta Journal* about a new book about Alexander. Nowhere in the article did it allude to Alexander's homosexuality, and Hephaestion was not even mentioned. When I read my letter in class, the other students took exception to me calling the omission a "conspiracy of silence surrounding gays and lesbians." No amount of explaining could convince these students that gays and lesbians were often left out of history. The members of the class insisted that there was no way to prove that Alexander was a homosexual. They argued that including this information would have made the article salacious. They stated that they didn't want to know about the "proclivities" of authors or historical figures. Even Dr. Probst thought this letter went too far.

The class discussion that day left me frustrated and made me wonder if LGBTQ issues would ever be included in the school curriculum. Clearly, the people in the class were not overtly homophobic. They had supported many of the letters I had read about LGBTQ issues, but they also were not ready to be honest about historical figures whose sexuality had been white washed by mainstream historians. While this discussion was frustrating, the assignment for the class started a letter writing campaign on my part that lasted for years.

One of my last papers that I had written for the specialist degree was for Dr. Many's class, and she called me into her office and asked me if I wanted her to help me get it published. I didn't take her up on it because I wanted to use it as part of my dissertation. I knew by that time that I would try to get a doctoral degree, and I feared that I wouldn't be allowed to use something that had already been published. But Dr. Many's belief in me was incredibly affirming. More importantly, Dr. Many's support was typical of the way all the professors had treated me during my pursuit of my specialist degree. I saw that at least at Georgia State, there were people who were ready to discuss these issues.

GLSTN

The controversy over the AIDS Awareness Week at Dryden showed me how vulnerable lesbian and gay teachers were in the school system. Administrators, even good ones like Mr. Robertson, relied on our fear of being fired to keep us silent. The administrators weren't necessarily against having lesbian and gay teachers on staff. On the contrary, in many ways they probably preferred it. Lesbian and gay teachers at the time rarely had children of their own as most heterosexual teachers did, and so they were often able to direct their full attention to doing the job. Michael, the drama teacher, provided a good example of this. He often was one of the first people to arrive at the school, and during drama productions, he often didn't leave school until ten or eleven at night. Many of the lesbian and gay teachers at Dryden were some of the prime contributors to the school. This is not to say that a few heterosexual teachers, like June, didn't put in a similar level of work. However, most heterosexual teachers, rightly so, had to direct the majority of their attention to their family.

As much as the school enjoyed getting the benefit of the dedication of lesbian and gay teachers, they also probably preferred that we stay in the closet. Many parents were very hostile to LGBTQ rights, and it was much easier for the school to have a "Don't ask, don't tell" policy with regard to lesbian and gay teachers. The fact that I could be fired without any other cause other than the fact that I was gay went from a fleeting thought to a constant presence.

After the incident with the AIDS Awareness Week, Janice and I started to talk about the need for lesbian and gay teachers to stick together and perhaps have some type of group to provide solidarity. Just prior to these discussions, while shopping at Outwrite Books I had discovered a book by Kevin Jennings, *One Teacher in Ten*. Jennings, who was originally from the South, had edited a book that included the experiences of lesbian and gay teachers from around the country. In the preface to the book, Jennings lamented the fact that he couldn't find any teachers in the South willing to contribute an essay. I wrote Jennings a letter thanking him for his book, but at the same time telling him that I would have been glad to contribute.

To my surprise, Jennings responded to my letter, and we began a correspondence about growing up gay in the South and about the group he had formed to bring lesbian and gay teachers together. He informed me of an upcoming GLSTN, the Gay, Lesbian, Straight, Teachers' Network, conference that would be taking place in the summer. He expressed interest in my attending the conference because he was eager to have someone from the South participate for the first time. It was too late for me to apply for scholarships that were awarded to participants, but I was only too glad to pay my own way. I was eager to see what this group had to offer. Janice and I felt that this would at least give us some indication of the possibilities available to us.

The conference took place in Philadelphia. My initial excitement about the conference began to diminish on the first day. Much of the morning was devoted to how GLSTN members should present an image to the public. There was a great deal made about how the media treated events by looking for the most extreme participants to take pictures of or to interview. We were instructed on how we might counter this by making sure that the media only had opportunities to photograph or interview participants who presented a conservative image. We were to try to eliminate any opportunities for the media to have access to drag queens or people dressed in leather. I thought that the LGBTQ movement had passed the point where we needed to have men in suits and women in dresses. One of the youngest members of the group did speak out against this policy, citing the fact that it was drag queens and people in leather who made the Stonewall Riots happen. But it was clear that the organizers of the conference and the overwhelming majority of the participants agreed that drag queens and leather people were an embarrassment and shouldn't be allowed to speak on behalf of teachers.

Given the history of gay rights in this country, I found this to be somewhat surprising. I was insulted and considered leaving the conference early. I called Anthony and talked it over with him. I also talked to another participant in the conference. Alan and I had immediately become friends, and he was also bothered by the discussion that had taken place. Unlike me, he had attended many GLSTN events in the past and assured me that this was not common. By the afternoon, I had written a letter to Jennings expressing my disappointment. Jennings and I later had a discussion about my feelings, and I expressed my admiration for the drag queens, leather people, and ACT-UP members who often were jeered at, spat on, and sometimes attacked in an attempt to fight for LGBTQ rights. I came to believe that there was a more radical side to Jennings that he felt he had to suppress in order to ensure the success of this group.

I stayed at the conference with the idea that I could at least get ideas on how to start my own group unaffiliated with the national group. As the conference continued, I felt that I was learning a great deal about how to get a group started. I also saw clearly how being a member of a national organization could provide us with many advantages we would never have with a local group. More importantly, I started developing friendships with the other participants in the group that would help me as I started trying to form an Atlanta chapter.

By the time the conference was over, I was determined to start a group when I got back to Atlanta.

ATLANTA CHAPTER OF GLSTN

As soon as I got back, I spoke with Janice, and we set out to start the GLSTN chapter. Janice and her partner, Lisa, both agreed to be members. I spoke with my friend, Ben Crosby, and he agreed to join. Janice and I didn't have as much luck when we started asking other gay and lesbian teachers who worked with us at Dryden.

When I approached Michael and Ford about joining the group, they were horrified. Ford flat out refused and wondered why I would even propose such a thing. Michael launched into a diatribe about how younger gay men didn't respect older gay men and that he felt that ageism was more of a problem that needed to be solved in the gay community than any problems involving lesbian and gay teachers. I could see clearly that starting a chapter was going to be more difficult than I originally thought.

I was determined to go on with my plan nevertheless. I looked around for a place to meet, and after a great deal of searching, the only thing I could come up with was the Gay Center. They would only allow us to meet for a fee, and this started my practice of paying all the expenses for the group. I found a way to attach a separate line to my own phone line that could be used as a phone number for the group. I contacted the *Southern Voice*, and I placed one of the free ads they offered to community groups.

The first meeting consisted of Janice, Lisa, Ben, myself and only one member who had been attracted by the ad, Becky England. Looking back on it now, I am surprised I didn't get discouraged, but the thought never occurred to any of us. We all knew that there must be dozens of other lesbian and gay teachers who felt the same way we did, and it was just a matter of finding them.

Our first order of business was finding places to meet and finding ways to get the news out that our group existed. Again, the Southern Voice came to the rescue. With just a call informing them that we existed, they immediately decided to run a story on us. I was interviewed for the article and my picture appeared. By this point, I was less concerned about people in the school system finding out that I was gay. Once the article came out, calls immediately started coming in from people who wanted to join the group.

Through his connections with ACT-UP and the activist

Jeff Graham, Anthony found us a place to meet free of charge, and very quickly we had established ourselves as a group. Although we had gained more members, most of them were reluctant to take a very active role. That left me to do most of the work, and many weeks I spent 20 hours or more on top of my full-time job trying to make sure the group got off the ground.

One of my tasks was to check the voice mail each evening, and it wasn't long before I got a call from a student. Daniel informed me that he had tried to form a Gay Straight Alliance at his school, but his principal wouldn't allow it. He had gotten the number for GLSTN from a woman he knew. This woman was a straight woman, but she had become very involved as a local gay activist during the disputes over the Cobb County ordinance banning homosexuals from the county. Daniel told me that she didn't want to get involved because she was a friend of his principal and often played tennis with her.

I told Daniel about the Equal Access Act. I had learned about the act during a talk by the lawyer for Lambda Legal Defense when he spoke at the GLSTN conference. The act had originally been lobbied for by Christian conservatives who wanted to ensure that students would be able to form prayer groups. Gay Straight Alliances were now using the act to make sure that they were allowed to form a school group. The act states that as long as a school allows any non-curriculum based group to form, it must allow all groups to form. The only way to deny a Gay Straight Alliance would be to also deny any Christian clubs or any clubs that weren't directly tied to curriculum.

Daniel was very excited when I informed him of the

law. He didn't feel comfortable bringing it up on his own, and he asked me to call his principal. I promised I would make the call. Although I agreed to call, I was somewhat nervous about it. I had no idea whether Daniel's principal would know my principal, and I worried about the problems I might be causing for myself in the school system.

The next day, I called Daniel's principal during my planning period. To my surprise Daniel was in her office when I called. She put me on speaker phone, and it seemed to me that she was clearly trying to intimidate Daniel throughout the conversation:

"Mr. Fair, what school do you work for?"

"Dryden High School."

"Well, I told Daniel that I wanted to look into the club before I decided whether to allow the club or not."

"You have to allow the club. The Equal Access Act demands that you allow the club unless you want to shut down all the other clubs in the school."

"Do you want Daniel to be responsible for us shutting down all the other clubs in the school? Do you think that would be safe for him?"

"I don't like the insinuation that Daniel wouldn't be safe. We might go about this a different way and bring some protests to your school over this. I don't think that would look too great for you."

"Look, I don't like these threats. I always intended to let Daniel form his club. I just have to figure out the best way to go about it."

"Great. That's all we are hoping for. Daniel, let me know what happens, and if you need my help, just call."

Daniel called me later to thank me for the phone call. I

encouraged him to get the *Southern Voice* to do a story about what he was doing so that other LGBTQ kids could know that a club like this could be possible. After a couple of days, he called me back and told me that his principal and the activist he knew had told him that it would be best if he kept the club quiet at first because board members might force it to shut down. He also told me that the activist had warned him that I was trying to use him to promote my group. I can see why the activist would have this concern, but nothing was further from the truth. I was disappointed because I thought this was quite a victory for LGBTQ high school students in Georgia and might be a model for other students, but I told Daniel that he should do whatever he felt most comfortable with.

Several months later, Daniel had his group up and running, and the activist was taking him to meetings of her group and touting her success with aiding Daniel in his efforts. Looking back on it later, I now realize that while Daniel was getting his group going, undoubtedly this activist gave him advice and helped him with various aspects of organizing a group. However, at the time it struck me as complete hypocrisy on her part. She, the person with nothing to lose, didn't want to confront the principal, and I, with everything to lose, did. I am sure that her perceptions of these events were quite different from my own, but at the time, to me it was more evidence of how the mainstream gay activists took advantage of the more marginalized members of the community. I was still glad that I had been able to help Daniel and that we had shown the principal that she couldn't use her authority to intimidate a gay student. It also showed me that even a very small group could have a great impact.

This was brought home to me in an even more powerful way later that year. A student, Tom Kameika, called the GLSTN voice mail. He was being harassed by a group of students at his school, and the administrators told him that it was his own fault. They said that if he hadn't let anyone know that he was gay, he wouldn't be harassed by the other kids.

School was out for the day by the time I got the message, but I took a chance that an administrator actually would still be there and would take my call. When I reached the administrator, I was surprised by the conversation that took place:

"Hello. Is an administrator available?"

"I'm an administrator."

"I'm Randy Fair with the Atlanta Chapter of the Gay, Lesbian, Straight Teachers Network. I'm calling about the recent incident with Tom Kameika. He has informed me that he is being harassed, and that you said it was his fault."

"What group are you with?"

"The Atlanta Chapter of the Gay, Lesbian, Straight Teachers Network."

"Are you a teacher?"

"Yes."

"What school do you teach at?"

"Dryden High School."

"Who is the principal there?

"Robert Robertson."

"Hmmm. Well, I did tell Tom that it was his fault. If he hadn't opened up his mouth about being gay, these boys wouldn't be harassing him. He should have kept his mouth shut."

"Look, you are responsible to keep Tom safe. No one should be allowed to harass and bully a student for any reason."

"He should have kept his mouth shut."

"Tom says that you didn't discipline the students who were bullying him."

"I'm not going to discuss discipline with you."

"That's fine, but this may all come out. If Tom continues to be bullied, we might have to organize a protest of your school. People might want to investigate the way you did or did not discipline the students who are bullying Tom.

"What group are you with and where do you teach?"

"I teach at Dryden High School, and the group is the Atlanta Chapter of the Gay, Lesbian, Straight Teachers Network."

"I will talk to Tom about all this tomorrow."

It was clear to me from the tone in the administrator's voice that he was worried about the attention that the LGBTQ community might bring to his school. The next day, he called Tom into the office and told him the harassment would be taken care of. The administrator then called in the students who were bullying Tom and told them of the possible punishments that they might face if they continued. Tom called me to thank me and told me that the bullying had stopped. He was able to finish the school year in what was at least a safer environment.

I realized after this event that just having the organization was important. These principals had no idea that our entire group consisted of fewer than twenty members. Just as they could use their power to intimidate students and teachers, we could use our power to intimidate them into doing the right thing. While I might worry that I would lose my job each time I would make one of these calls, they would worry that at any time our group could call on the larger LGBTQ community to protest and bring unwanted attention to what they were doing.

As the year went on, I was proud of our first year with the Atlanta chapter of GLSTN. We had increased the membership to 15 to 20 people, participated in the Back to School campaign sponsored by the national organization, and had helped at least a couple of students along the way. As spring approached, I started to plan the first conference for our chapter. Once we got the group started, various other groups would ask me to attend their meetings when the focus had anything to do with schools, and I planned to use these new connections to provide speakers for the conference.

I attended meetings for the Parents and Friends of Lesbians and Gays, meetings of gay parent groups, church meetings devoted to helping gay youth, Youth Pride events, etc. Through these meetings, I had gotten to know many of the local activists who were dedicated to helping LGBTQ youth, and more importantly, I knew their credentials and areas of expertise. These people, like most LGBTQ activists at the time, were willing to give freely of themselves for the greater cause.

For the conference, I had gotten: Judy Colb, President of Parents and Friends of Lesbians and Gays; Sarah Lynne Chestnutt, Director of the Office of Lesbian, Gay, Bisexual Life at Emory University; Barbara Budd, Collin Quinn, Stephanie Swan, and Linda Wilson: therapists who worked with LGBTQ youth; Judy Gerber, President of the Lesbian, Gay, Parents' Association; Marty Avant, President of the Decatur/Dekalb Gay Straight Alliance; and Stephanie Swan, Director of Youth Pride. I was very proud of this group of speakers and excited about what they would bring to the conference.

The willingness of these local experts made organizing the conference much easier, but I had no idea of the problems I would face as the project continued. The first thing I needed to do was find a space for the event. Someone had suggested that I call the Friend's School, a Quaker school in nearby Decatur. Since I was funding virtually everything the group did by myself, this meant that I needed to find some place that was free. To my surprise, the principal of the school almost immediately agreed to host the conference. He told me of the Quakers' commitment to social justice, and he let me know which date we could use for the event.

I proceeded to get the speakers to commit to that date, and I got the schedule prepared. My next task was to get publicity for the event. Both *Etc.* magazine and the *Southern Voice* agreed to do a story about the event, but they couldn't donate advertising. I went to gay businesses to see if I could get them to co-sponsor the conference in return for them donating money for the ad. Although everyone agreed it was a good cause, no one would co-sponsor the event. Bev Cook, the manager for the Heretic, a local bar, said the bar wouldn't sponsor us so she took seventy-five dollars of her own money out of her pocket and volunteered it. When I couldn't find anyone else to do the same, I gave her back her money and decided to buy the ad myself. I couldn't afford an ad in the *Southern Voice* since it would cost at least four times the amount for the ad in *Etc.* So, I took out the ad in *Etc.*, and Janice designed the ad for me. The Etc. was much more of a bar rag than a newspaper, but it had the advantage of being more widely distributed. Many members of the GLSTN chapter expressed their dissatisfaction for the ad because they felt that Etc. was not a respectable news magazine. They worried about our ad being in a magazine that included ads that had sexually suggestive content. They preferred the *Southern Voice* which they felt was more mainstream.

This was not the first time I had encountered criticism of this type. Janice and I had arranged social gatherings for the group at a local bar. Our regular meetings often only dealt with the business matters of the group. Janice and I wanted a chance for lesbian and gay teachers to have a chance to socialize, and we wanted to broaden our reach to as many lesbian and gay teachers as possible. We thought that there would be some lesbian and gay teachers who would be interested in a social setting but who might not feel completely comfortable joining the group. Some members of the group felt it was inappropriate for teachers to meet at a bar, and they brought their complaints to me. As with all the complaints, I ignored them.

As I continued organizing the conference, I was getting used to criticism, but I was surprised when the next chastisement came from Kevin Jennings. When I went over the schedule of speakers with him, he became somewhat upset. He scolded me for not consulting with him and told me that he had always planned to bring a representative from Lambda Legal Defense with him to be one of the keynote speakers. He also wanted to bring in some big-name speakers he had in mind that would garner more attention than the local speakers. He insisted that without some bigger names, we wouldn't be able to attract people from throughout the South. When he had originally agreed to speak at the conference, he hadn't mentioned anything about guest speakers. He also hadn't mentioned that he wanted the Atlanta chapter to pay for these speakers. Other than some very token membership dues, I was the sole source of income for our chapter. I didn't have thousands of dollars to pay for big name speakers. Kevin insisted that we would make a lot of money by increasing attendance, and we would make all the money back.

In addition to being unhappy with the list of speakers, Kevin was also upset about the location of the conference. He wanted the conference to take place somewhere in the downtown area of Atlanta, not out in the suburbs of Decatur. He had in mind the conference room of a hotel. I understood his point that a downtown venue would be easier for participants to get to and big-name speakers would draw more attention, but I also understood that a free space and free speakers would be a great start for our first year.

In frustration, I finally ended any debate on the matter by telling him that the Atlanta chapter would have our own conference without any help or participation from the national organization. Kevin had really wanted to establish a chapter in the South because the national organization had not had any success in getting a chapter going in the region until we started our chapter. He agreed to come to the event under my original plans, and he also had the national chapter pick up the expense for the speaker from

Lambda Legal Defense. I immediately changed the schedule of speakers to accommodate these new speakers.

The most upsetting challenge I faced in organizing the event came from the principal of the Friends School. After getting everything in place for the meeting, I called him to go over the list of speakers. He immediately told me that we couldn't hold the conference at the school. I was shocked, and even more shocked when I learned the reason. He hadn't told me when I originally asked about using the school that he wanted the conference to involve gay and lesbian students. It turned out that the school had received a grant from a gay group, and part of the grant involved the school being able to show that they had done work with lesbian and gay youth. He saw my conference as a way to get his grant.

I thought the Friends School was offering to host the conference for completely altruistic reasons. I had no idea they needed the event to fulfill a requirement. I spent a week looking for a new place to host the event. In the process of looking, I told a prominent gay activist in town about the situation. Phillip Rush told me he would talk with the principal but assured me that he couldn't make the principal host the event. I don't know what, if anything, Phillip said to the principal, but the principal called me and offered a compromise. He agreed that we could hold the event at the school, but we would need to have speakers from Youth Pride as part of the day's agenda. I readily agreed to this, and once again, I adjusted the schedule of speakers.

Finally, with all the petty problems out of the way, the conference took place on May 4, 1996. Several teachers from Dryden came to the conference to support me, and even Lily, the lesbian assistant principal, and her partner came. The conference was a huge success as far as I was concerned. Janice had printed up some beautiful programs and made t-shirts for us to sell to raise money, the school was scenic and beautiful, and about sixty participants showed up. Most of the participants were lesbian or gay, but there were a few straight people in attendance. June was one of the teachers from Dryden who came and so was my friend, Clare.

When it was time for the Youth Pride members to speak, June and I watched with shock as the typically stoic Clare began crying during the students' presentation. While there really wasn't a dry eye in the house, none of us had ever seen Clare cry. The principal of the Friends School, with his demand that we have the speakers from Youth Pride, had actually helped make the conference a success. I was happy when Lily and her partner were impressed with the conference. Lily and I were often at odds over my approach to LGBTQ issues at the school. I felt that she could see for the first time why I was speaking up the way I was. Prior to this, I felt that she thought that my outspokenness at school had put all the lesbian and gay faculty in danger.

By the end of the conference, everyone seemed pleased with the day. Many of the participants had made contacts with other people who shared their interests, and we were all reminded of why we were doing this work. Kevin told me that this conference, more than any other he had ever been to, reminded him of the first conference GLSTN had ever had. I felt great about what we had accomplished, and I could see that this was something that could grow throughout the year.

Earlier, during one of the breaks in the conference, Kevin asked me to meet with a representative from The Southern Fund for Communities. This was a group closely connected with Coretta Scott King, and they gave grants to Southern grassroots organizations working to promote human rights. The national organization had used our chapter as evidence that they were beginning to establish chapters in the Southeast.

It turned out that I vaguely knew the man in charge from seeing him at protests throughout the years. I went over what the group had accomplished for the year, and I was a little apologetic that we hadn't done even more. Kevin assured me that we were doing more than most active chapters that had been around for years, and the representative from The Southern Fund said that he was impressed with what we had accomplished in just a year's time.

Based on the success of our chapter, we were awarded $3500. I certainly didn't expect the national organization to give us all of that, but even $1000 of it would have given us a huge increase in our budget. We had started to create a small budget by this time, both from membership dues and the little bit of profit we made from the conference. Kevin informed me that we wouldn't be eligible for any of the money because the national organization had initiated the grant request. He did tell me that the national organization would provide one scholarship to the national conference, so at least the person we sent wouldn't have to pay his or her way like I had the previous year. I was frustrated with the national organization. I am sure they felt they had done a lot for us by providing Kevin and David Buckle from Lambda as speakers for the conference, but I felt they could have done more to help our chapter. I was once again disappointed by what I saw as the mainstream activists.

By the time Gay Pride came about that summer, we had built the group to about thirty members, and I was very hopeful. I knew that the parade gave us a chance to raise the awareness of our group, and I felt certain that the many teachers who had never heard of our group would see us and would want to join. In the early planning stages, I had grandiose ideas of what we could accomplish. I imagined us somehow getting a school bus to drive in the parade and passing out apples to the crowd with a GLSTN sticker on them. Much to my dismay, I soon discovered that the only member of the group willing to march in the parade was my friend, Ben Crosby. I even offered the possibility of members marching with bags over their heads as I had seen some teachers do in other gay parades around the country. But really, wearing a bag over your head during June in Atlanta isn't that wise, so I wasn't really surprised when no one took me up on it.

I had hoped that some of the core group of members would have a change of heart. Things had been moving forward in other areas as far as the group was concerned. Steve Epstein, someone I had known for almost the entire time I had lived in Atlanta, had agreed to attend the national conference. Although Steve agreed to go to the conference, he felt that he couldn't march with us in the parade. It was his first-year teaching, and he didn't want to take a chance on getting fired if seen marching.

Even with everyone refusing to march, I refused to give up on Gay Pride. We did have many members who agreed to work the tent for the festival, but I was determined that we would somehow march. With no members, other than Ben, I decided to enlist my friends to pose as teachers. Ben, Fran Soloman, Anthony Ricciardi, Gregg Holloway, Gene Carnes, and I all marched together with a sign that I had purchased (once again using my own money). Even with our tiny group, people noticed us. As soon as one person in the crowd would read our sign, they would begin nudging the people beside them saying, "Look, a group of teachers." The cheers we received were some of the loudest for any group in the parade, and we had lesbian and gay teachers run out into the street to ask us how they could find out more about our group.

The march had worked out just as I had hoped. By the end of the weekend, we had over 100 potential new members signed up. Finally, I saw our group taking off.

Steve went to the national conference in July, and when he got back, he immediately told me that he wanted to take over as co-chair of the group. He said that at the conference Kevin had told the participants that if they were unhappy with the officers in their chapter, they should get rid of them and take their place. I called Kevin to tell him how I felt about the situation. Kevin seemed surprised and explained to me that he was talking about chapters that had become ineffective, and that he certainly had no idea that Steve would think that he meant our chapter.

I had been going to school to get my specialist degree, and I had already made up my mind that I wanted to get a doctoral degree. I was tired of putting so much time into GLSTN in addition to teaching full-time, and I definitely wanted more of the members to step up and take more of an active role in the group. Janice had already decided to step down as co-chair, and eventually Jana Jackson stepped up to take her place.

We had a meeting of the officers (Steve was treasurer at the time), and he repeated that he wanted to take over my spot as co-chair. He had decided to quit teaching and work on GLSTN full-time. I was curious about how that would work, but his dad had died and left him a small inheritance. He assured us that he felt that this work was so important that he felt it deserved someone who could do it full-time. I couldn't disagree with that.

Some of the other officers felt that I had been too assertive in carrying out activities for the chapter and hadn't asked for their approval in advance. I couldn't deny this charge since it seemed that I always had difficulty getting even the other officers to take an active role in most of the activities. I agreed that I would step down as co-chair, and the other officers asked me what I would like to do with the organization.

The most important thing we had done that year, in my opinion, was the conference. I said that I would like to still be in charge of organizing the conference. They agreed to that, but said that I would have to get everything approved by them before I committed to anything. I explained that it would be virtually impossible to do that because the process was so complex it required immediate decisions. I knew how difficult it was to get all of the speakers to commit to a certain date from my previous experience, not to mention getting a place, ads, workers, etc. They wouldn't agree to this, and so I stepped aside and let the others take over the group.

Kevin called me to express his disappointment, and he was angry with me that I didn't try harder to remain co-chair. I was happy to let someone else deal with everything and ready to invest my time in my doctoral program. Steve took over, and with his personality and good looks, it wasn't long before the membership of the group really took off.

Steve asked me to help out periodically with the group, but he made it clear that they no longer needed me as an active member. Looking back on it now, I realize that I needed to break free of regular membership in the group. While I might have complained about getting very little help from the others in the group, my taking control of every event gave them every reason to not step up and take more of the responsibility. I had been co-chair of the organization for a year and a half at that point, and I probably couldn't have remained much longer.

I was becoming disillusioned with the group, both on a local level and a national level. It seemed to me that the LGBTQ community itself had changed. When I first moved to Atlanta, the core group of out gay people was so small that we were entirely supportive of each other. We knew that the enemy came from the outside, not from within. I expected a certain amount of criticism for decisions I made, and I could easily dismiss the people who complained about the ad in *Etc.* or about our social gatherings at bars. However, some in the group had started to criticize my personal life. At the time, I was dating Guy Meyers. Guy was the well-known female impersonator, Felicity Fahrenheit. He performed with two male dancers who wore very skimpy clothes, and together they were known as Felicity Fahrenheit and the Degrees. Some members of GLSTN thought it was unseemly to have the co-chair of a teachers' group dating a drag queen. This was completely anathema to what I thought the LGBTQ community stood for.

With regard to my relationship with the national chapter, I was also becoming disturbed by the path they appeared to be on. When I had argued with them about the donation from The Southern Fund and about the guest speakers for the conference, I had started to notice that the focus often seemed to be on raising money rather than changing policy or attitudes. Adding to this feeling was the changing of the organization's name. The national organization decided they would no longer be called the Gay, Lesbian, Straight Teachers Network, and instead they would now go by the name, the Gay, Lesbian, Straight Education Network. The reason the national organization gave for the change had to do with fundraising. They explained that many donors didn't feel strongly about giving money to a group that focused on teachers, but they would give money if the focus were broadened to include education in general. I understood their point, but one of the greatest things about the group for me was its focus on teachers. I felt like I had seen this with many gay groups over the years. They started out at the grassroots level and were really focused on doing great things. Because people did support the noble reasons for the group's existence, they started to grow larger and larger. The bigger they got, the more money they needed to keep going. Volunteer positions turned into paid jobs. A vicious cycle began where the more money they raised, the more money they required. After a while, it seemed that their sole purpose became raising money. I watched this play out with the newly named GLSEN in just the way that I knew that it would.

Buoyed by the success of the Atlanta chapter, the national organization decided to create the job of regional director for the Southeastern region. This position was supposed to create many chapters of GLSEN throughout the South. I knew that this was unlikely to work. Southerners are often wary of people who come from outside the region to make changes in their way of life. The very reason that the Atlanta chapter had success was that we started as a grassroots organization.

With Steve in charge of the local chapter, more of the other members started taking more active roles, and the Atlanta chapter was having a great deal of success. Steve was incredibly good looking and had a gregarious personality that was hard to resist. He increased membership and made GLSEN one of the most active and well known of all the LGBTQ groups in the city. Steve was a master at getting positive publicity, and the next year, they had the type of conference that Kevin had wanted, a large conference with big name speakers at a prominent downtown hotel. They asked me to present at one of the sessions, and I agreed.

Things seemed like they were going incredibly well for the first few years. Steve had quit his teaching job and worked full-time on the group. The group seemed destined to be a success.

Then, Steve got into a dispute with the national chapter. Accusations of mismanagement of funds were made by the national organization, and they told the Atlanta chapter that they could no longer be affiliated with GLSEN. Members of the local chapter asked Steve to step down and tried to keep the organization going, but in a relatively short time, the group ceased to exist altogether.

I was bothered by the collapse of the group, but at the same time, I knew that it was one of the risks I took by walking away and letting other people take control of what I had started.

OTHER SCHOOL CONTROVERSIES

While I was busy working with GLSTN, I was still working as a teacher full-time. In my school system, teachers always went back a week before the students. The week is spent planning and getting rooms ready, but it is also used for professional development. Never had that been more true than when Lily was assistant principal. Each summer she went to conferences or seminars, and she couldn't wait to bring all of these new ideas to the teachers at Dryden.

During the '96–97 school year, Lily had gotten a speaker from the Anti-Defamation League to kick off the professional development. The previous year we had some racial tension at the school. This racial tension was kicked off when a group of white boys at the end of the school day had taken it upon themselves to go out and get a gigantic Confederate flag and drive around the school parking lot in their pickup truck waving the flag. Some of the African-American students had decided to retaliate, and they challenged some of the white kids who were involved to a fight. The fight was broken up by administrators and teachers before it ever really got started, but the hostility hung over the school for the entire year.

A speaker from the Anti-Defamation League was chosen in part to address this hostility. She was an African-American woman, and in her speech, she mentioned virtually every possible group that could be discriminated against except LGBTQ people. She also used humor throughout her speech, and one of the jokes that I took particular offense to was when she told us all that she was looking for a "BMW," and went on to explain that this stood for a "black man walking." During the speech she announced that during the upcoming year, the Anti-Defamation League would conduct diversity training for selected students who had been identified as school leaders.

I was sitting next to Michael and Ford during the speech, and all throughout the speech, they kept mentioning that she hadn't said anything about LGBTQ people. To be fair, Michael always loved nothing more than to instigate things. Michael and Ford wanted me to be the one to confront the speaker. I didn't need much encouragement, and I approached her after her speech. Ford and Michael had followed me so they could listen to what I said:

"Thank you for your talk. I have some concerns about it though."

"What are your concerns?"

"Well, first, I didn't like the joke about the black man walking. You are the Anti-Defamation League, and I think that people who aren't ambulatory might take offense to that joke."

"Wow. You really don't have much of a sense of humor do you? I guess you are right that it could be seen as insensitive, but it's just a joke."

"My next objection is the fact that you didn't even bring up gay and lesbian kids. You mentioned every group except that group."

"We will bring that up in the workshops with the students, but we never bring up that group in our talks or in the literature we give out because the parents would be against it."

"Don't you think that's a little hypocritical?"

"We have to sneak that topic in. If we don't sneak it in, parents would be against the entire program. We wouldn't be able to do workshops at all. Do you think it would be better for us to leave it out altogether or hide it temporarily in order to get it into the schools?"

"I actually do think it would be better for you to leave it out altogether. The way you are doing it now gives validation to the idea that this is so bad that it needs to remain secretive.

"Well, I have to disagree with that."

Seeing that I would get nowhere with my argument, I walked off. I wrote a letter to the organization addressing my concerns and got a similar response from the leaders of the Anti-Defamation League.

The Anti-Defamation League did its work with students, and much of the school year became devoted to multiculturalism. Later in the year, Michael, as the director of the drama program, conducted a diversity presentation in which members of the drama department talked about things that made them "different." The program was one of the most moving things I have ever seen in a high school setting. Students talked about a variety of things that had caused them to be discriminated against. Some of these differences involved ethnicity, but others were things such as weight or other characteristics. One girl decided to come out as a lesbian.

As the weeks leading up to the presentation got closer,

she approached Michael and said that she felt she had to speak up. She had originally planned to do a skit about her identity as an African-American woman. However, as rehearsals went on, and she heard more and more students talk about their own experiences with discrimination, she felt that she wanted to talk about how much she felt discriminated against as a lesbian. Michael was worried that her revelation could cause him problems, so he decided he needed to get approval from the administrators beforehand. He talked to the administrators, and they said he would need approval from the girl's parents. The girl told her parents that she wasn't a lesbian, but she would merely be playing the part for the benefit of the show. Her parents agreed, and she was allowed to present her skit.

The young woman's presentation created a sensation at the school in the sense that for that day it seemed that all the students wanted to discuss it. Surprisingly, to me at least, the students were very supportive of the girl. Many of them defended her by insisting that she was merely acting, but even those who felt she was not really a lesbian said that it wouldn't matter to them either way.

After the program was over, many parents were outraged that she was allowed to come out at the presentation. They called the school to complain, and even called the superintendent's office, but of course, the presentation had already taken place, so there was little they could do about it. The parents saw this presentation as the school's attempt to promote a liberal agenda.

Many of the parents at Dryden were huge fans of Rush Limbaugh. His radio show was incredibly popular at the time, and one of his favorite topics was the liberal teacher with an agenda. With that in mind, there was a small group of parents who were eager to make this case. I grew angry every time someone made the charge of liberal teachers promoting an agenda. While the conservative parents who made these complaints could only see this from their perspective, from my perspective, it was, more often than not, conservative teachers who promoted an agenda. So while the issue the conservative parents had with the multicultural program died down, I could see other issues that no one in the school seemed willing to address. One example of this happened with the senior newsletter.

The senior newsletter was a single page front and back flyer that contained information of events and tasks of importance to seniors. Distributed in homeroom, it gave seniors knowledge of scholarship opportunities, special events for seniors, and other things of that nature. When making these newsletters, the person in charge almost always found him or herself with extra space that needed to be filled.

At this time the counselor responsible for producing the senior newsletter was a very conservative woman. I really liked her, and she was a wonderful counselor. However, when she found herself with extra space, she would include quotations from one of her favorite political pundits, Cal Thomas, an extreme right-wing political columnist. These quotes went as far as stating that the separation of church and state was not created to protect the state from the church, but instead to protect the church from the state. In one particular quote Thomas suggested that the church should be involved in schools, especially in the issue of prayer.

Now, in truth, very few students paid attention to even the important information in the newsletter, and even fewer students read the quotes used as fillers. I only discovered the quotes when a student pointed them out to me. Certainly, I had no problem with teachers, or any other school employee, sharing their political or religious preference. In later years, when a teacher put up a life size poster of George Bush during the presidential campaign, I had no problem with it, despite the administration's threat to the rest of us to not share our political views during the campaign.

However, the senior newsletter struck me as something different. The newsletter was a publication that all seniors at least theoretically needed to make themselves familiar with. I found the senior newsletter to be different from the school newspaper. There was no opportunity for dissent in the senior newsletter as there would be in the school newspaper or a classroom discussion.

When I brought this to the attention of Mr. Lusk, the principal at the time, I did it by sending an email pointing out the quote and saying, "I don't think the senior newsletter is the place for quotes from extreme right-wing political columnists." To my surprise, he responded in what almost seemed like an attack with an email saying, "The senior newsletter isn't the place for left wing quotes." I was taken aback, but I responded to his email by saying, "I couldn't agree with you more. The quotes, in my opinion, should be historical in nature, perhaps famous quotes from Jefferson, Lincoln, etc. I don't think the quotes should be from the left or the right and based on current politics." Mr. Lusk never responded to that email, but the political quotes were not included after that point.

This is a small, seemingly insignificant incident, but it does illustrate the difficulties that face LGBTQ teachers and liberal teachers as well. While the counselor who put the quotes in the paper faced no disciplinary action, an LGBTQ teacher would have most likely been threatened with job loss or at least some lesser disciplinary action. From my experience, LGBTQ teachers were always suspected of promoting an agenda. This accusation was virtually never considered for conservative heterosexual teachers even when it was clear that a personal agenda was at work.

When the issue of standing up for the flag came up at Dryden over the years, I saw this certitude on the part of conservative teachers that their viewpoint was not only the correct one but the only possibility. Each time this occurred, the teachers demanding that students stand up for the pledge defended their position by saying that they were teaching patriotism. There was never the least notion on their part that they were promoting an agenda.

In one of the incidents that took place at Dryden, one of the teachers who was arguing with me about the pledge insisted, "I think these kids should be made to stand up. I am very patriotic. I support the military. There are people dying right now defending this country, and these kids should be made to stand up."

I replied, "So you think that people in the military are dying for the right to force students to stand up and say something they don't believe. That is what we criticize other countries for. I thought that in America you are supposed to be able to believe whatever you like." She replied, "Well. These kids should be made to stand up."

When I pointed out to teachers that it was illegal to force students to say the pledge, they informed me that they didn't care about the law. They insisted that the law was wrong and stated that allowing students to not say the pledge encouraged disobedience.

I can't imagine an LGBTQ teacher going this far in asserting an "agenda." Of course, these teachers who were asserting their point about standing up for the pledge subscribed to the majority opinion. They in no way believed they were promoting a point of view. They were, therefore, rarely ever questioned, and on the rare occasions when they were challenged, they reacted with surprise and disbelief.

I witnessed a perfect example of this when I was working on my dissertation. As part of my study, I needed to observe teachers' classes. The English teachers at Dryden were very generous to allow me to observe even though they knew that I might have to be critical of some of the things they were doing.

One of the teachers I observed had won teacher of the year after only three years of teaching. The other teachers, her students, and I all agreed that she was an excellent teacher doing a wonderful job. On the day I needed to observe, she was conducting a grammar class. I thought it was unfortunate that I had chosen a day for grammar because I thought the class would be so impersonal I wouldn't have anything significant for my research.

Much to my surprise, her grammar lesson was one of the most personalized lessons I had ever seen. She started out talking about the subject and verb. She said, "The subject and verb work like a team. It is like my husband and me. We are a team. We work together. Caroline, I saw

you and your boyfriend at the mall. You two are a team."
The lesson went on with personal examples throughout. I
watched in awe because I knew that the way she was
teaching grammar would really stick with the students for
years to come.

However, there was no awareness on her part that her
lesson was reifying heteronormative values. Her examples
offered only the traditional family structure as a model. I
was further shocked when she started teaching the
comma, semicolon, and period. She said to the class, "I
always think of the semicolon as the female period." My
face went flush. The rest of the class had been so personal
that I thought for a moment that she was going to compare
the period to a woman's menstrual cycle.

What happened was almost as bad. She said, "I always
think of the semicolon as the female period because a
semicolon is used when the sentences are closely related.
It is kind of like a female because you know how gossipy
girls are. A period is more like a male because it is kind of
to itself." I stared in amazement at her analogy. She
noticed the look that came over me because she said, "Mr.
Fair, you probably think this is very sexist, but that is just
the way I have always been able to remember it." I sat in
silence because I didn't want to contradict her in her
classroom, but I did think it was very sexist.

My observation of her class made me wonder just how
commonplace discussions like this are in the school
system. She clearly recognized her sexism, not that she
was going to change it. However, she didn't even recognize
how heterosexist she was being. Since she didn't recognize
it, she didn't think she was promoting any agenda, but of
course she was.

This was the same with my teachers when I was in high school, and with the other very traditional and conservative teachers I have witnessed over the years. Their political views were embedded in the lesson in subtle ways.

The uncomfortable truth is that, as teachers, everything we do is fraught with politics. From the moment we decide which textbook or which works we will use with the students until the final test, everything is imbued with politics. With this in mind, I always believed that it was better to let students know my political point of view so that students were better able to question whether or not I was being biased.

Dryden at the time was a part of the same district that had elected Newt Gingrich to the House. The area was overwhelmingly Republican and overwhelmingly Christian. Often, students who had any point of view that varied from the consensus of the community were afraid to speak up. I became even more convinced that it was important that I give voice to this minority opinion.

Because the students were aware of my politics, a group of students approached me to sponsor their newly formed club. They called themselves, SOFTI, the Society of Free-Thinking Individuals. The students in the club were for the most part the school's misfits. They dressed differently, wore their hair differently, and most importantly thought differently than the overwhelming majority of the other students. I was glad to give these students who didn't feel accepted at the school a place where for at least an hour they could find other students like themselves.

One of the young women in the group stood out

because unlike most of the other members, she was extremely popular. Sophie's popularity was in part because of her extremely charming personality and in part because she was strikingly beautiful. The most popular heterosexual males at the school wanted to be around her, and she was always very nice to them, but she preferred to be around the students in SOFTI because they shared the same point of view and liked similar things.

Several of these students were in my fourth period class. Because the fourth period also included lunch, an extra thirty minutes was automatically built into the class for a study hall period. The students rarely ever studied during study hall and instead used the time to socialize. I bonded early on with Sophie and her friends in part because I sponsored the SOFTI club, but I solidified that bond when I overheard the group's conversation one day. Sophie and her friends were very into tattoos and piercings. During the class, they were discussing this fascination and the talk progressed to a discussion of a Prince Albert. From my friendship with Anthony, I knew that a Prince Albert described a piercing of the penis. As the group started to leave for lunch, I stopped them and said, "I don't know if a Prince Albert is an appropriate discussion for school." Everyone in the group got embarrassed, and someone in the group said, "Oh no! He knows what it is." They told me they would be more aware in the future and make sure their conversations were appropriate.

When these same students visited Piedmont Park one weekend afternoon, I was the one who was embarrassed. Piedmont Park is in the heart of the city of Atlanta in the Midtown neighborhood, and I almost never saw students in the city. On the weekends, Piedmont Park was filled with gay men, and my friends and I went there frequently on the weekend. I was surprised on the Sunday afternoon when I saw my students in the park. Sophie was there with two of the males in the group and a student from another school in the area. I introduced them all to my friends, and we were having a conversation about why they had decided to come into the city. Another one of my acquaintances, a gay man, saw me and came over to say hello. When he got close enough to me, he gave me a quick kiss in greeting. He had no idea that these were my students. My face went red, and I looked at Sophie and her friends. Sophie had no reaction at all. The males looked at each other, shrugged their shoulders and continued talking as normal.

When I got home, I called June. I worried that this would create a controversy at school, and June assured me that it wouldn't. When I told my friend Ben about it, he laughed uncontrollably. Later he gave me a t-shirt with pictures of lesbian and gay couples kissing with the caption, "Every kiss is a revolution." The students must have thought nothing of the kiss because it never came up as an issue at school.

However, this incident reminded me of the vast difference between LGBTQ teachers and heterosexual ones. I rarely ever shared any kind of personal information with students, and I certainly would have never dreamed of talking about my relationships. The teacher whose grammar class I observed, not only was willing to share information about her relationships, she included these discussions as a regular part of the class.

SOUTHERN VOICE

One of the times where my personal and professional life did come into conflict with each other was because of my decision to write a column for the gay newspaper.

This was 1998, and as the LGBTQ community in Atlanta continued to grow and change, it got more mainstream and more conservative in its approach to politics. The people who were increasingly feeling free to be open about their sexuality were the ones who in the past had been passing as heterosexual, and more often than not, they felt very comfortable with mainstream society. Increasingly, the LGBTQ activists of the early years were being pushed aside by these newcomers to the community.

From my point of view, nowhere was this change more evident than in the workings of the *Southern Voice* newspaper. The paper had been started by a couple of lesbians who were dedicated to providing news to the community, and the paper was edgy and radical. By the late nineties, a group of affluent gay men got together and purchased the paper. As the paper grew in size, it became more mainstream and less open to what were now the fringes of the gay community.

More significantly, in order to gain more readers, the paper took a decidedly more conservative turn. The paper couldn't increase its growth by appealing to the community activists who were already readers, so they needed to appeal to the more conservative elements of the gay community who had shunned the paper previously.

In order to make this shift, Chris Crain, a Harvard grad, became the editor of the paper and brought on board many new columnists. My ACT-UP friend, Anthony, and I were extremely bothered by this change. In our minds, we couldn't help but wonder, "Where did these people come from?" Suddenly, the leading voices of the LGBTQ community in Atlanta were not people who we had seen doing the hard work of protesting for change. Now, these new voices seemed to suddenly emerge from nowhere. Oftentimes, the tone of the writing, especially in the editorial pages, clearly showed the discomfort these new writers felt towards what they viewed as the unseemly members of the community.

Nowhere was this more clear than in the writers' attitudes toward sexuality. For weeks on end, columns appeared criticizing gay men for their sexual practices. Granted, at least some of these editorials were meant as parody, but others were quite straightforward in their criticism of anything other than monogamous relationships. It was quite ironic that when lesbians owned the paper, they showed no embarrassment, but when gay men took over, suddenly they felt that the sexual practices of other gay men were hurting their attempts to be accepted by straight society.

After weeks of reading column after column of criticism, I wrote a very harsh letter to Crain. To Chris' credit, he didn't just ignore my letter although he didn't publish it either. He called me and asked me if we could meet. He said he wanted to talk about the letter I sent. When we finally met, he told me that not many things bothered him, but that his face went flush when he read my letter. I had written many letters to the editor of the *Southern Voice* even before Chris had become editor, and he complimented me on my writing style. We then had a long rambling conversation about politics that made me more puzzled by him than I already was. At the end of the conversation, he asked me to be a columnist for the *Southern Voice*. He told me that I could write on any topic that I liked and that he wouldn't censor me.

Once I had agreed to write the column, I felt that the first one should be something that would counter the judgmental attitude that other columnists had voiced. Chris decided to call my column, "Fair Game," and he gave this column the title, "Unsafe Sex No Reason to Condemn Promiscuity." I didn't love the title because I wasn't advocating unsafe sex, but I didn't object to it either. He included the byline, "Randy Fair is a school teacher and can be reached through this publication." We had argued when he wanted me to identify myself by saying the name of my school or at least the system. I wouldn't agree to it because I didn't want there to be any way that anyone could say that I was trying to represent Dryden High School or my school system.

The article came out on a Thursday, and by Friday at lunch, Michael and Ford were already talking about it at school. Michael told me that he thought I had guts because he never would have written the article, and Ford refrained from talking much about the content, instead focusing on the fact that I was now a columnist for the paper.

I hadn't worried too much about others seeing the column. This was in the days before the internet had really caught on, and the *Southern Voice* wasn't published online. In addition to that, the paper was really only distributed in the city, and Dryden was far out in the suburbs.

I, of course, knew there was possibility that someone from the school system could stumble across it, but I didn't imagine people reading the *Southern Voice* unless they were LGBTQ themselves or were LGBTQ friendly. Since the article was public knowledge, naturally Michael and Ford started talking to other teachers about it. On Monday, I had a note in my box saying the principal wanted to meet with me at the end of the school day. At that time, we had an interim principal who was just filling in. No one would tell me what the principal wanted, but of course, I suspected it had something to do with the article.

When I went into the principal's office, he told me that he needed to get an assistant principal to sit in. He didn't get Lily, the assistant principal who was a lesbian, he got Chuck. Chuck was a great assistant principal, but I knew that the principal had chosen him because, of the four assistant principals, Chuck was the one who was considered by everyone on staff to be "the good ole country boy." Once Chuck got into the office, the principal dramatically opened his desk drawer and pulled out a copy of the article and a faxed letter from a parent.

I read the letter and looked at the article. The letter was not only sent to the superintendent, it was also sent to the president of the PTSA. The principal asked me if I had anything to say. I responded, "What do you want me to say? It has my name on it and my picture. I wrote it."

"Look, your lifestyle is your business, but if parents and ministers in the area get wind of this, we might have to transfer you or terminate you."

"I think you need to know that I was the co-chair of the Atlanta Chapter of the Gay, Lesbian, Straight Teachers Network. I have attended lots of seminars on the legal rights of gay and lesbian teachers. I also told the former principal when I started that group, so I think that I am within my First Amendment rights."

"I understand, but the superintendent wanted me to call you in. If ministers in the area or parents hear about this, students may become disruptive in your class. If they do, we probably won't be able to control these discipline problems. We probably won't terminate you. We will probably transfer you, and it probably won't be anywhere you want to go like Springdale. It will be somewhere like Riverside or Lakeview."

Anyone who knew of the county school system in that time would know that this was clearly a racist comment. Springdale, like Dryden was predominately white and Riverside and Lakeview were predominately African-American. The irony in what he was saying was that I had taught at Riverside before coming to Dryden, and every year at Dryden, I had asked for a transfer to Lakeview.

At this point, he told me that the PTSA president wasn't going to say anything about the article (I had taught her daughter the previous year) and that both he and Chuck would not mention the article to anyone. He told me that I shouldn't say anything about it to anyone either, and that we should hope the whole thing would blow over. He said that June had been in his office trying to find out what he wanted with me, but that he wouldn't tell her and that I shouldn't tell her or anyone else. He also told me that I should not write any more columns. I shook his hand and left the office.

I was very shaken, and immediately went to talk to June. June already knew about it because Lily had told her what was going on, but she hadn't said anything to me because Lily had asked her not to. She told me that she was going to call some people she knew in the downtown office and see what she could find out.

As soon as I got home from school, I immediately called Lambda Legal Defense. It was not a day that they normally took legal questions, but the secretary could tell how upset I was, and he put me on hold. Steve Scarborough, the lawyer for Lambda, answered my call even though technically I should have been asked to call back on a day when they took intake requests. Steve spent hours on the phone with me and told me that I should immediately write down what happened so that I would have a record if we had to go to court. He also instructed me to mail my report to myself, get it postmarked, and leave it sealed. He wanted us to be able to open it in court to show that this was my recollection of the conference immediately after the event. He spent even more time with me advising me of my legal rights.

Anthony and our friend, Anne Louise came and got me to take me to dinner. On the way, we stopped off at Outwrite bookstore, a gay bookstore, and I got a copy of Karen Harbeck's book *Gay and Lesbian Educators: Personal Freedoms, Public Constraints*. When we got back, unable to sleep, I read part of Harbeck's book. I discovered from Harbeck's research that many lesbian and gay educators bought into the myth that the school system was right to fire them simply for being gay. I also learned that many, if not most, lesbian and gay teachers were threatened at some point in their career with dismissal. Harbeck made the point that usually these cases were settled out of court and a gag order was often part of the settlement, so even in the many cases where the lesbian or gay teacher won, the perception was that the teacher had lost the case. From reading Harbeck, I quickly realized that the threats made towards lesbian and gay teachers were often made with no real desire to fire the teacher. Instead, they were made to ensure that the teacher kept quiet.

The next day at school, Lily called me into her office. She wanted to talk about the column and asked me what the principal had said. She proceeded to tell me that from her talks with people in the central office, it was suggested that I should stop writing the column for the Southern Voice, remain quiet about the situation, and let the whole thing blow over. I told her that I had no intention of stopping the column, and that if the school system wanted to pursue it I was willing to take it to court. I flippantly said that it had always been my dream to sue the school system and retire early. I told her that unlike other lesbian and gay teachers I had read about, I would not agree to settle the case out of court even if it meant losing the case. "If the school system wants to see its name in The Atlanta Constitution every day, so be it."

I knew that Lily would tell her partner and the other people she knew in the central office, and I knew that they would likely be worried about bringing negative publicity to the school system. Although I didn't make a threat about other issues that I could bring to public knowledge, I am sure that the "powers that be" were worried about my bringing these additional issues to light. This was one of the biggest factors in my feeling that the officials from the school system were being very hypocritical about the entire situation.

Many students and most teachers who attended Dryden High School at the time were aware of various "scandals" that had taken place at the school. These issues had occurred before I started working at the school, but they were well known and included teachers drinking on the job and having relationships with students.

I can understand why the column caused controversy with the school officials, but it was in a newspaper intended for adults and was merely the expression of an idea. The incidents with the heterosexual teachers were actions that really did have an impact on the school and the community. These "indiscretions" were discussed, but no one even considered threatening to fire any of them.

I don't know what possessed the people at the central office to drop the issue. It could be that they felt is was easier to let it drop than risk having the negative publicity. It could have been that June, Lily and my friend Ben, who had numerous connections with the people in the downtown offices, worked on my behalf and talked them into dropping it. It could have been that they never intended to take any action, but were merely trying to scare me into stopping the column. Whatever the reason, I never heard from them about the issue after that initial meeting.

Lily discussed the issue with me one more time and told me that if I intended to continue with the column, I should avoid any issues that dealt with sex. I told her, "When I write my column, I will deal with the issues of the day. If the issues of the day have nothing to do with sex, I won't mention sex. If the issues of the day have to do with sex, then my column will deal with sex."

For all the criticism about the column, I had many more positive reactions from gay men who thanked me for bringing this issue out in the open. A psychologist who lived in the same condo building with me was one these men. He worked with gay clients, and he told me that the article had been brought up in a group session, and it gave the group a chance to have one of their most productive discussions that they had ever had. The topic had been so taboo that no one in the group had the courage to bring it up previously. Numerous other gay men told me that this column had given them a chance to speak honestly with friends about their own feelings on the issue.

A NEW PRINCIPAL

The next year, we had a new principal at Dryden, Ken Lusk. On the opening day, Mr. Lusk gave a beautiful speech about his views on education, and in my opinion, his speech showed a desire to move the school culture in a more academic direction. He also showed a compassion for students that was reassuring, and he demonstrated a love of intellectual ideas. After his speech, I approached him and asked if we could meet. He said that he would be pretty busy in the opening weeks, but he would try to make time. I asked him if we could just talk as he walked towards his office, and he agreed. I briefly told him about my work with GLSTN and informed him that I wrote for the *Southern Voice* (by that time I was a regular columnist). I told him that I wanted him to know about this so that he wouldn't be caught off guard if someone brought it up later. He said that he appreciated me telling him and that he was glad that gay students had someone on staff who could provide support. I felt very good about my decision to tell him. I would have gone into more details about the specifics of the column, but since I was only able to talk with him during our walk towards his office, I cut the story short.

Along with getting a new principal that year, we also got a new assistant principal, and a man who had been a teacher and a coach was given a job as an administrative assistant (a sort of assistant principal in waiting). The assistant principal came in promising us that he was a strong disciplinarian and that he had no intention of letting students get away with anything.

Mr. Lusk, as part of his attempts to make the school more academically oriented, was adamant that he wanted students to be in class for the full hour, and so he wanted teachers to be more stringent in enforcing the tardy policy. We were given strict instructions that students should be given a warning on their first tardy, on the second they should be given a detention with the teacher and their parents should be called, and on the third tardy, they should be turned over to the administrator for discipline. If they didn't show up for the private detention, they were also to be turned over to the administrators.

It wasn't long before I discovered that the new assistant principal and the new administrative assistant had no intention of following these rules when it came to my classes. Since they were following through with the other teachers' students, I had to assume this was somehow related to their homophobia. When I turned in students for the third tardy, both of these administrators would encourage the students to say that I hadn't called their parents, or when I would turn them in for not coming to the private detention, the administrators would send a note telling me that the student had a legitimate excuse for not showing up and so deserved a second chance. When I confronted the administrators about the third tardy referrals, they would say the student said I had never called the parent. When I would show the log recording the date and time of the calls to the parent, they would say it was too late because they had already met with the student.

As some students began to realize that these two administrators were not going to enforce the rules for my class, I started to encounter more and more defiant behavior. As the year went on, some students had forty or more tardies to class and still had never received any punishment. I still did not have a lot of discipline problems, but as spring came around, I had one female student who kept using the phrase, "That's so gay," in a pejorative sense. I asked her to stop, but she continued to do it over the next few days.

Finally, I referred her to the office. The assistant principal wrote on the referral sheet that he had met with her, but he didn't write any punishment. Over the next few days, she would go out of her way to use the phrase again. I referred her to the office each time, and each time she came back and said that the assistant principal had laughed about it. That same year, the governor of Georgia, in an effort to get tough with discipline in schools, had ushered in a law allowing teachers to dismiss students from class if they continued to misbehave. The understanding was that they would not be allowed to return unless the behavior changed.

I first went to the assistant principal:

"I turned Kathleen in a few times for using inappropriate language, and she says that you laughed about it. I'm not going to allow her back in the class until her behavior changes."

"She's going back to your class. I met with her, and she hasn't done anything wrong."

"No, she isn't coming back to class as long as she continues to use that language."

"She has a First Amendment right to say whatever she wants. She hasn't violated any rules. She will be back in class."

I might have accepted that as an answer if the student had been using the comment as a political statement or was using it as a comment about curriculum, but clearly this wasn't the case. I had certainly had many students in the past say that homosexuality was immoral or disgusting to them, and I hadn't referred any of them to the office because that was well within their first amendment rights. When I countered that she was in violation of the rules for failing to follow the teacher's instruction, he laughed about it and told me that he had no intention of disciplining the student.

After I spoke with him, I immediately went into Mr. Lusk's office and reported the incident. To Mr. Lusk's credit, he immediately called the assistant principal into his office, had me repeat what the problem with the student was, and informed the assistant principal that this would not be tolerated at Dryden High School. He told the assistant principal to make it clear to the student that she was to return to class and follow my instructions from this point forward.

After that I didn't have any further problems with the student, but the assistant principal and administrative assistant had made it clear how they felt about having a gay teacher at the school. I was lucky to have Mr. Lusk on my side. If I hadn't had help from him, the discipline in my classes might have deteriorated, and I can even see the possibility that if the discipline had become a problem, I might have been fired. The experience I had made me wonder how many lesbian and gay teachers have been driven out of the classroom through a similar process.

GSU

During this same time period, I had decided to return to Georgia State to work on my doctorate. During my work on my specialist degree, I had followed my rule of always turning whatever the assignment was into an opportunity to focus on LGBTQ issues. I never had the slightest problem with any of my papers. Every professor had been completely supportive, and I intended to continue this policy for my doctoral degree.

When I went for the interview for the doctoral program, I got the same supportive reaction that I had seen previously at Georgia State. All the professors were excited by the fact that before I had even started the program I knew what my dissertation was going to focus on. One of the professors even tried to get me to change my area of interest and move to his department, leadership. I told him that I wasn't interested because, unlike teachers, administrators didn't have tenure. Administrators could be fired for any reason or no reason, and I knew that from my column to my activist endeavors, my outspokenness could easily cause the end of my career. As the interview came to an end, Peggy Albers, a new professor at Georgia State, immediately told me that she wanted to be my advisor because she was interested in LGBTQ issues.

The support I received at GSU was amazing until I got to Otis Winston's class. I was excited to take Dr. Winston's class because he was somewhat of a legend at Georgia State. The students who had taken his class raved about his teaching, and he had a list of published works that could rival anyone's. From the first class, I could see why his reputation was so strong. Not only was he extremely intelligent, but he was an amazing teacher. He was one of the most dynamic teachers I have ever seen.

The title of the class was Psychology of the Inner-City Child. He explained to us on the first day that the term "inner city" was a euphemism for African-American and went on to explain that when he started at Georgia State they wouldn't let him use the words African-American studies, so instead, they always replaced the word African-American with the word "inner city children." All the assignments listed in the syllabus made it clear that we were to focus on the problems of inner-city students. Dr. Winston also made it clear in that first class that due to changing demographics this did not necessarily mean that we had to do our projects exclusively on African-Americans, but instead we might choose any group that was a part of the urban school system.

It was very typical in my experience at Georgia State that on the first day of class the professor would have everyone in the class say their name and what they were working on. We did this on the first day of class in Dr. Winston's class as well. Dr. Winston would make a remark or two after each person's statement. When it got to my turn, I said, "I'm Randy Fair, and I am working on why literature teachers teach the works of lesbian and gay authors but don't tell the students that the author is lesbian or gay." I was met with a stony silence. After a few moments of complete quiet in the room, we went on to the next person.

One of the assignments for the students in the class was to add to an extensive, annotated bibliography Dr. Winston had developed over the years. The subject of this bibliography was African-American studies, and not surprisingly, there was not a single book on the list that dealt with issues facing LGBTQ African-Americans. Even though I knew at this point that Dr. Winston would not be receptive to it, I decided to add to the list with books that dealt with the issues facing LGBTQ African-Americans. At that time, even the Georgia State library was lacking in books on the subject. Phillip, the owner of Outwrite Bookstore, let me use his store to gather the information I needed. I turned the bibliography in, and Dr. Winston gave me an A for the assignment, but I was sure that he wouldn't add these works to the bibliography.

At that time, we also had to announce what the subject of our final paper would be. When I said that I would do mine on the difficulties faced by LGBTQ teens, he told me in front of the class that I couldn't do that as a topic because it didn't meet the requirements of the class due to the fact that it didn't have anything to do with inner city children. He went on to the next person, and that gave me the rest of the class to think about how I would respond.

I waited until the class was over and everyone else had finished talking with him, and I walked out with him.

"Dr. Winston, I am going to go ahead with my topic for

my paper."

"You can't do that. It doesn't have anything to do with urban students, and the syllabus makes it clear that the paper has to be about urban students. Gay kids are in all schools, so that won't qualify as a problem facing inner city children."

"African-Americans, Asian-Americans, and Latino Americans are in all schools also. Students who live in the inner city are more likely to see other lesbians and gay people and may therefore be more likely to 'come out' while still in high school, and so that qualifies this as an inner-city issue."

"You know when I was in high school, we had a gay teacher in the school. All the kids knew that the band teacher was gay. He was a great teacher, but he kept quiet about it, so we respected him. That's the way it was back then. It was much better when everyone kept their mouth shut. I don't want you to do your paper on this topic."

"I'm sorry, but I will be going on with the paper. If you don't accept the paper, I am going to take it up with the affirmative action office."

Georgia State had just added sexual orientation to its non-discrimination clause, and I was determined that I wouldn't be silenced. One of the things I found so surprising about his stance on this topic was the fact that his statement about being quiet reminded me of what Southern whites often said about African-Americans. When we finished the conversation, he had not given any indication as to whether he would accept the paper or not, but I went home and continued to work on the paper as I had planned. I worried the entire time that I might not receive a good grade on this one, and I had made an A in every class throughout the program, but I was determined to go ahead with it no matter what the grade.

Another requirement of the course was that we had to present the findings of our paper to the class. From this presentation, I learned very quickly just how much the teacher sets the tone for the rest of the class. In other classes at Georgia State, I had met with little resistance. This class was clearly an audience that was opposed to me before I ever started speaking. With the other presenters, class members clapped when they finished and asked questions. When I was done, no one clapped or asked a single question. Dr. Winston quickly moved on to the next student.

I turned the paper in as planned, and when I got it back, I had again made an A, but written on the front cover was this note:

Randy,

This is a fascinating paper, well written, and a penetrating analysis. An in-depth treatment of your topic area. It is very informative and deals with a significant education issue. As you show, many of the elements of the model I shared apply to this issue.

I still have some reservations about the fit of the topic in the "inner city" child class. As I indicated earlier, "inner city" initially was a euphemism for African-Americans as an ethnic group. Later, other "inner city" ethnic groups were included as an option for special circumstances, but with the clear intent to keep the primary focus of the class on African-Americans as an ethnic group.

While oppression is a part of the African-American experience, the main focus is ethnicity as primary identity, recognizing of course that there are many aspects to the African experience including gender or gay and lesbian issues.

Oh well, this is a long-winded explanation. Even so, your treatment of the topic is excellent. You have helped me to clarify the focus of the course. You are a top-notch student.

Otis

This letter was extremely troubling to me because I admired Dr. Winston so much as a teacher. As intelligent as I knew him to be, I knew that he couldn't possibly believe that it was possible to separate identity based on ethnicity and say that it was more important than an LGBTQ identity. More troubling to me was the statement, "You have helped me to clarify the focus of the course." From other conversations I had with Dr. Winston, I knew this meant he would change his syllabus to make sure that no one ever did another paper like mine. This was nothing short of hypocrisy because for years he had allowed people to do papers that had nothing to do with African-Americans as long as they focused on other ethnic groups that existed in inner city schools. When Dr. Winston's name came up with other students, I never mentioned anything about my experience except to say what an incredible professor he was. Despite my experience, I still had the utmost respect for both his scholarship and his ability to teach.

I had the exact opposite experience in Susan Talburt's class. Like Dr. Winston, Dr. Talburt was someone whose name I kept hearing over and over again. As with Dr. Winston, everyone was completely impressed with her, and they kept mentioning her to me because she was one of the very few "out" lesbians on the faculty. The fact that she was in the education department made this fact even more impressive.

I first met Dr. Talburt when Dr. Many gave us an assignment that involved interacting with a professor who shared the same field of interest and keeping a journal of the interactions. Even though Dr. Talburt had never taught me and didn't even know me, she graciously agreed to an email conversation about my dissertation work. I literally spent hours writing my emails, and she went out of her way by spending hours responding.

When it was time to register for the next semester, I made sure I signed up for Dr. Talburt's class. Like Dr. Winston's class, Dr. Talburt's class also had around 35 students in it. This high number of students was unusual for graduate classes. Unlike Dr. Winston's class, however, there were four or five other lesbian and gay students in the class. In Dr. Talburt's class, there was no moment of discomfort when on the first day I announced my dissertation topic. Other students had already announced similar topics.

After the first day, the topic of LGBTQ studies didn't come up again in the class because none of the works we studied dealt with the issue. This, of course, had been true in Dr. Winston's class as well. However, in Dr. Winston's class, any time I made a comment in the class, I was uncomfortable. In Dr. Talburt's class I felt completely confident when I joined in the discussion.

Nothing could have made the role of the attitude of the instructor more clear to me than these two experiences. The more I reflected on this difference between the two situations, the more I realized how this might apply to the high school setting as well. It clearly illustrated for me the tone that could be set by the instructor's attitude.

As I thought about other classes I took at Georgia State, I realized that the fact that the professors were more than accepting of me and my research had made the students more willing to see my presence as acceptable. When the professors interacted with me in positive ways, the students in the class reacted in positive ways. Even when the other students disagreed with my point, they always showed respect for my comments. Any disagreements they had with me came from a philosophical or intellectual point of view and not from a personal antipathy to me.

When I encountered homophobia from other students, it was rare and subtle. One case of this subtle homophobia was with a student who had taken several classes with me. While one of our professors was lecturing, she wrote me a note telling me that I talked about gay issues too much. She went on to say that she understood why I talked about it because she knew that if I didn't talk about it, no one else would bring it up. But she said that she worried that people might start to think that gay issues were the only things that I could talk about. I wrote her back explaining that just as she and her friend who was also in the class couched their responses to things from the point of view of their experiences as African-Americans, I couched my responses from the point of view of my experiences as a gay man. I gave her a few examples of how she had done this with some of her responses. Her response to me was that people expected her to talk about her experiences as an African-American, but they were uncomfortable by hearing about the experiences of a gay man.

While I did occasionally encounter some of these small incidents of homophobia, more often than not, the other students were completely supportive. In one class, after giving my topic, I was surrounded by other students during the break. They wanted me to know how happy they were that I was working on this topic. One of these students was Suzanne Anastasi. Suzanne was working on studies involving Hispanic and Latino issues in the school system, and we immediately bonded over the similarities in our research. Suzanne was one of my biggest supporters throughout the program, and it reassured me to have other students who were on my side.

VAXGEN AND VALENTINE'S DAY

As I continued to teach and take classes at night, there would be new ways that my personal life would intersect with my professional life. When this happened, it always made me think about the pressure that the school system places on both LGBTQ teachers and students. One such incident happened when I decided to be a part of a drug trial.

While I was working on my doctorate, the pharmaceutical company Vaxgen was working with the AIDS Research Consortium of Atlanta on testing an experimental AIDS vaccine. It just so happened that one of the sites they had chosen to explain the research behind the testing was on the campus of Georgia State. Since the seminar was being held just as one of my classes was ending, I decided to go and find out more.

As I sat there listening to the scientific reasoning behind this experiment, I became more and more convinced that I should participate. When I thought of the death of my first boyfriend, Mark, the fact that now my two best friends were positive, and the countless lives that might be saved, there was no way I couldn't go through with it. I had always wondered how it could be possible that I lived through the years when the disease was raging through the gay community, and yet somehow I had survived. With that in mind, there was really no decision to be made. I had no idea how this seemingly completely personal decision would involve my school life as much as it did. As far as being a participant, I would remain anonymous throughout the experience, so seemingly no one would need to know.

However, as soon as I made up my mind to start the vaccine trial, I realized I had to let at least some people at school know because of the testing times. One of the reasons that I decided to go ahead with the vaccine trial was that most of the appointments took place at the beginning of the process, which just happened to correspond with spring break and summer break. I knew that I would be able to make all of these appointments with no problem. However, as the trial went on, I would have to make 4:30 appointments periodically throughout the school year. Knowing that I would have to leave school five to ten minutes early on the days I had appointments, I had to tell June what I was doing and ask her or another

English teacher to cover the last part of my class from time to time so that I could make the appointments.

June surprised me by being against my participation when she first heard about it. She didn't think I should use my body for experimental purposes. I explained to her the scientific reasoning behind the study, and finished by saying, "If everyone had the attitude that they don't want to be the one to go through the experiment, then these experiments could never take place." Once June saw that my mind was made up, as she had always done in the past, she gave me her full support. She agreed to cover the last minutes of my class whenever I needed to go to the appointments.

As the vaccine trial went on, I realized that there would be other times that the subject would come up at the school. One of those times involved the annual blood drive. Someone on the faculty decided to start doing blood donation drives at the school. One of the greatest things about teaching at Dryden for all those years was the sheer number of charities that were supported by the members of the school community. Because of age requirements, only senior students and teachers could give blood. When they started promoting the blood drives, students immediately began asking if I was going to give blood.

I could have lied or simply told them that I wasn't giving because of personal reasons, but I felt it would be more educational to explain to them the true reason. I felt that this would give them a chance to see how scientific research was conducted and explain why even though I normally participated in every cause, I could no longer give blood. When I told the students about the vaccine trial, there were numerous reactions that covered the entire range of possible feelings. A few students thought it was a great thing to do. Other students thought that I was crazy to participate in such a study, and other students thought I must be HIV-positive. Of course, they didn't phrase it in that way. Instead, they would say, "So you have AIDS?" I would have to explain that having AIDS and being HIV-positive are two different things and that my participation in the study couldn't be possible if I were HIV-positive.

Although I wasn't extremely concerned about negative consequences for revealing my participation in the study, in the back of my mind, I did have a little bit of fear that some parents might overreact to my involvement in the vaccine trial. I had seen a very small minority of parents act in foolish ways before, but overall, the parents in the Dryden community were incredibly accepting.

I didn't get any complaints from either parents or students about my participation in the study, but one student did tell me that his mother said I must be promiscuous or I wouldn't have been able to participate in the study. These occasional personal revelations were always another reminder of how different the experience of a gay teacher could be from that of a straight teacher. I could walk into virtually any classroom of a straight teacher and see pictures of a wife or husband. No one thought of this as promoting heterosexuality or calling attention to one's sexuality. I could observe classes, and teachers would constantly mention things they did with their spouse as metaphors or examples of something they were teaching. No one thought of this as inappropriate even when it wasn't directly related to curriculum. However, gay teachers constantly had to be aware of sharing details of their personal life in the classroom, and there were constant instances where the personal and the professional would intersect.

My experience in school with the Vaxgen trial made me reflect more deeply on some of the more subtle ways heteronormative values function in the school system. While at times it might have been a source of annoyance for me, for LGBTQ students it had to be positively confounding.

I started to realize that some of the events that were a part of the school culture were possible sources of stress for LGBTQ students. Obviously, homecoming and the prom could potentially be difficult times for these students. But it was the celebration of Valentine's Day that bothered me the most of all the annual events. Every year for Valentine's day, various school groups took advantage of the holiday to raise funds. One way they did this was by selling roses and other flowers that would be delivered in homeroom. It seemed to me that most of the other adults at school couldn't see how harmful this could be for both straight and LGBTQ students. Typically, a few young women would receive a multitude of flowers and candy on Valentine's day while other female students received none. Each year during homeroom, the teacher had to give out the Valentines that had been purchased for the students. Every year, I felt for the girls who didn't receive flowers or candy. Not only did I feel bad about the obvious stratification of the homeroom on the basis of popularity, I also felt bad about the fact that LGBTQ kids couldn't show their affection for partners in this way. While on the surface it seems like a trivial thing, it was one more example of how LGBTQ kids had to remain secretive about who they loved.

Even worse than the distribution of flowers was the annual Valentine Computer Match. The Future Business Leaders of America each year sponsored a computer match where after filling out a personality survey, the students would get a list of the ten most suitable "matches" of the opposite sex. No one ever stopped to think about the LGBTQ kids or to think about how much this reinforced heterosexual norms. Whenever I would point it out, even other gay teachers would treat me as if I were crazy. To them it seemed like a perfectly normal part of the adolescent experience.

There were numerous occasions such as this that continued to come up over the years. Because LGBTQ students were invisible, no one stopped to think about these situations that reinforced the view that heterosexuality was the only option.

EMMA

For me, being a gay teacher caused a constant awareness of situations that would occur throughout the day. There were numerous times when I had to decide how to negotiate the path between maintaining my self-respect and making sure I retained my job. One such experience involved a student named Emma.

Although I had continued to use June's idea of talking about a newspaper article of the day as the opening activity of the class, as time went on, I added other ways of using newspaper articles as a part of the class. I would sometimes break students into small groups and give them an article about a controversial issue. In their groups, they would have to determine the reasons that the people on each side of the issue felt that their point of view was correct. I also began to give bonus points to students who would write letters to the editor regarding the article. They would get even more points if their article was published.

Over a period of five years, I had literally over a hundred students get their letters to the editor published. Sometimes it would be a surprise to me to see which letters The Atlanta Constitution decided to publish. But more often than not, I could tell which letter would be published the minute I read it. One letter that I knew would be published as soon as I read it was written by one of my best students, Emma. The letter Emma had written dealt with the issue of girls and body image. She had written a moving letter and had personalized the issue by talking about how she felt about her own body. She even went as far as to talk about the fact that she was made to feel uncomfortable because of what she viewed as her small breasts.

When I read the letter, I immediately thought how courageous she was to talk so frankly about something that most girls would never openly discuss. By the time I read the letter, it had already been sent, otherwise I might have reminded her that this letter would enter the public discourse for everyone to see. Anytime a letter was published, I read the letter to each of my classes. I hesitated to read Emma's letter to the classes. I felt that her letter was so personal that it might be best if I didn't read it. But if I didn't read it, I believed it would make the letter stand out even more. I decided to ask Emma before reading her letter to the classes, and since it was in the paper for everyone to see, Emma said she didn't mind. When I read the paper to the classes, the girls immediately began discussing the issue of body image and how difficult it was for them. Even though the girls were supporting the same ideas that Emma had brought up in her letter, Emma became a little angry with me for reading it because it brought attention to the very thing that she was self-conscious about.

My reading of the letter caused Emma to be a little pouty for a while as teenagers can often be, but I just assumed that her bad mood would wear off as the school year went on. That moodiness turned into anger later in the year when Emma tried to turn in a paper exceedingly late. I felt that she was deliberately turning the paper in late to instigate an argument with me. She was always so meticulous with every assignment that I found it hard to believe that she didn't have this composition when it was due. Even though she was one of my best writers, I couldn't make an exception in her case because I had given other students reduced grades on their papers when they had been late. The amount of points that I penalized Emma was really more of a token punishment. It didn't change the A she always maintained in the class.

At that time, we were on block schedules, which meant that classes were two hours long with several minutes between each class. I was in a portable classroom for much of my teaching career, and during the break between classes, I had run inside to run off some copies. When I returned to the classroom just before the bell rang to start class, someone had written on the board in very large letters, "Randy is a Homosexual." I simply erased the board.

Luckily for me, the students were taking a test that day, so I gave out the test and had some time to think about how I would address the situation. I knew that I wasn't going to let this incident pass, but I didn't know exactly how I should approach it. I knew that if I got mad and chastised the students about it, the students would think that being homosexual was something to be ashamed of. If I ignored it, they would think that being a homosexual was so bad it couldn't be discussed under any circumstances.

At the end of the class, I told the students that I wanted to talk about what had happened at the beginning of class. I reminded them of our reading of The Contender the previous quarter. I asked them to recall that at the time we were reading the novel, I told them that there were going to be some inappropriate words used to describe Jewish people and African-Americans. I prompted them to remember the caveat I had given before their reading took place. I had explained at the time that the author was using these terms to make the book realistic in terms of the way street language might be used by the characters. I also reminded them that before condemning the author for the use of those words, it was important to try to understand why the writer was using these terms.

Using that discussion as my analogy, I said again that it was just as important for me to try to perceive the intent of the author of the message on the board. Then, I told them that I was having a problem trying to address the writing on the board because if I said it was wrong, then they would think there is something bad about pointing out that someone is homosexual when we wouldn't think there was anything bad about pointing out that someone was heterosexual. Then, I pointed out that it was clear that whoever had written on the board intended to hurt me with the words. I said that I expected an apology from whoever had written it.

At the time, I suspected that it was one member of a group of boys who sat in the back and were always in trouble for one reason or another. I was surprised later in the day when Emma came back to my class to deliver a note of apology. She had tears in her eyes and was shaking a little as she handed me the paper. In her note, she had explained that she was angry about the fact that I took points off her late paper, and she wanted to do something to get back at me. The rest of the letter apologized profusely.

Emma went on for the rest of the year to be the great student she had always been, and surprisingly the rest of the class was even better behaved. Unlike many other gay teachers I have known, I had relatively few incidents of harassment from students. However, I have observed other LGBTQ teachers who have had students write derogatory comments all over the desks or leave hostile and threatening notes. These incidents are always a struggle for an LGBTQ teacher. In many ways, lesbian and gay teachers during the time period I taught were somewhat faced with the same struggles that the Mary Bryant, the African-American teacher from Riverside, encountered.

Although it began to change over time this was especially true of gay men in the school system. What I witnessed over at least half my career is that any time a student had a problem with a female teacher, the teacher was immediately categorized as a bitch. For much of my career, it seemed that when a student had a problem with a male teacher, the teacher was immediately categorized as a faggot. When I observed this occur with straight men, they immediately dismissed it because it wasn't personal to them. When it happened with gay men, they felt attacked on a personal level.

It is impossible to teach in the high school setting without hearing an endless stream of invectives. Even when I first started teaching, I told June that it surprised me that the majority of the curse words we have are either scatological or sexual in nature. It shows me that on some subconscious level we are completely uncomfortable with these natural acts.

Over the years, I saw the automatic characterization of males as faggot give way to the use of the word "dick" for every male teacher a student didn't like. When this pejorative wasn't used, the word "douchebag" started to gain traction. I had numerous arguments with students about the term "douchebag." When I said that it was sexist, the students would at first think I was insane. Since they weren't really even thinking about the words they used most of the time, they were surprised when I pointed out the connection of this word with a woman's personal hygiene and the discomfort the word conveys for our general feelings regarding something that is a natural part of being a woman.

One of the most difficult parts of teaching was searching for these underlying meanings in what happened. Whether it was Emma's writing on the board or the words the students regularly used, I tried to constantly look for the deeper problems these behaviors signified and tried to remember that often these problems were not the problem of the student, but the problem of our society in general.

MATTHEW SHEPARD

On October 9, 1998, I heard on the national news for the first time about the attack on Matthew Shepard. Although the attack took place on October 6, it took a while before it made the national news. It was a Friday night when I saw the news story for the first time, and I spent the rest of the weekend in my apartment contemplating what had happened. Despite the fact that I had kept up with the news since I was a very small child, this story hit me more than any other.

I guess what stunned me most about this story is what it said about us as a nation. I had heard of and protested against gay bashings that had taken place in Atlanta, but that was in the late eighties and early nineties. By the time the murder of Matthew Shepard took place, Midtown Atlanta, where I lived, was almost totally gay. It was very easy living in the comfort of Midtown to forget just how much people hated us. The Matthew Shepard story was a reminder of that hatred. I remember the feeling of powerlessness that was the most frustrating part of the emotions I felt that weekend.

As the weekend went on, I turned to writing. It occurred to me that I had been a *Southern Voice* columnist for a while at that point. I had letters and columns published in *The Atlanta Constitution*. Maybe the one thing I could do was write about my feelings. By the end of the weekend, I had written the following column that was published in *The Atlanta Journal* on October 19th:

I am haunted by the story of University of Wyoming student Matthew Shepard. This young, gay man was allegedly lured by two young men posing as gays and then was beaten, burned, and left for dead. Anyone who heard the story undoubtedly was shocked and horrified at the heinousness of this crime.

But this was not the only beating Matthew had endured. Friends report that because he was open about his sexual orientation, he had been attacked on two previous occasions.

I worry when I hear stories like this. I worry about the pain Matthew must have gone through before he was killed. More than that, though, I worry because sensational stories such as this allow us to keep an emotional distance.

Only the cruelest people will justify the homophobia involved in this crime. We can all feel superior to Matthew's alleged attackers because we have never beaten or killed anyone. Many people, however, verbally attack gays and lesbians on a regular basis.

As a teacher for the past 12 years, I cannot possibly count the number of times I have heard students in the halls call each other "fags" or "dykes." The phrase "that's so gay"—meaning something is bad or unworthy—is a part of almost every student's lexicon.

Teachers who would never allow a racial joke or epithet

often tolerate and sometimes even encourage humor and invectives against gays and lesbians. Every elementary school student knows that the worst name anyone can be called is gay.

If adolescents didn't learn this hatred for lesbians and gays in school, they would certainly pick it up through popular culture. Popular movies, television shows, and songs are filled with anti-gay rhetoric.

Russell Henderson and Aaron McKinney, Matthew's alleged attackers, learned the same lesson that everyone in our society learns from a very early age: gay people are horrible and don't deserve to live. It would not be surprising if these two came to this conclusion. Even our national leaders use gay-baiting to win elections.

The fact remains that the average person would not try to kill people because of their sexual orientation. Most gays and lesbians do not have to endure being beaten, burned and tied to a stake. However, if what I have witnessed in schools is anywhere near representative, most are verbally beaten and harassed every day.

Given this, it is no wonder that the suicide rate for lesbian and gay teenagers is three times higher than that of heterosexual adolescents. It is not surprising that gay teenagers are more likely to become addicted to drugs. It makes sense that gay and lesbian youths make up a very large percentage of runaways.

We can all condemn Matthew's alleged killers for the evil

that is in their hearts, but how many of us are just as guilty?

I hadn't intended to share the column with my students, but once it came out, several of them started telling me that they had seen it in the paper. A few of the teachers at Dryden posted the column in their rooms. The students who hadn't read it wanted to, and I had several students ask me if I would read the article to them. I thought that it would be a good example for the class. I felt that this would show them that rather than merely talking about the importance of writing, I actually did try to "practice what I preached." I read the article to the classes, and we briefly discussed the problem. About a week later, there were a couple of responses to my column in *The Atlanta Constitution*. I shared these with the students as well:

LESSON OF TOLERANCE

Thank you for running Randy Fair's very thoughtful column on the destructive effect of anti-gay rhetoric. The despicable actions of people who waved messages of hate at the funeral for gay student Matthew Shepard reflect the hatred for gays and lesbians that our society has tolerated and encouraged for too long. It matters very much what we teach our children. I am glad that Fair is one of the individuals who is teaching them.

—Sharon J. Strange Stepler (Lawrenceville)

HARASSMENT RARE

If schoolteacher Randy Fair is truthful when he claims to have witnessed daily verbal abuse and harassment of gays and lesbians, that revelation saddens me. However, in all my years attending public schools, I found such behavior rare. My wife, who has been a public school teacher for 25 years, agrees with this assessment. Perhaps Fair's statement that "everyone in our society learns from a very early age that gay people are horrible and don't deserve to live" reveals his misguided perception of homophobia.

—Charles H. Carpenter (Fayetteville)

The letter from Charles Carpenter caused more discussion in my classes than the original column. The students couldn't believe that someone would say that derogatory words against lesbians and gays were rare. They all commented on how frequently they heard these words each day. Even though there were other gay teachers at the school, this discussion and the column turned me even more into the gay teacher at the school.

In addition to changing the way students viewed me, I got numerous phone calls from parents who said that were dealing with the fact that they had a child who was being bullied at school. They wanted advice and wondered if they should press the administrators at the school to do more to stop it. All I could tell them was that if I were a parent, I would definitely force the administrators to stop the bullying.

The sheer number of people calling and writing to me after one column in the newspaper was proof to me of just how limited the resources were for people at the time. Being gay, I knew numerous resources for help with lesbian and gay issues. However, these straight parents had no way of knowing about these groups or these services.

SARAH

Each year there are certain students who stand out in the mind of the teacher. One of these students for me was a young woman named Sarah. While I was in graduate school, I had asked June to let me teach all ninth grade because with only one preparation I would be able to devote more of my time to my GSU classes. Dryden at that time was still a blend of the "old" Dryden community and the "new" Dryden community. The old Dryden community consisted of the people whose families had lived in the area for generations. They tended to be somewhat conservative and very proud to consider themselves as small town, rural people. The new Dryden community consisted of people who had moved from the North for job opportunities. These people, while still tending to be somewhat conservative, were more accustomed to embracing new ideas.

Sarah's family belonged to the "old" Dryden group, and she was very proud to embrace Southern culture and traditions. She was extremely bright, and I quickly saw that she was the best writer in the class. At the time, the people of the state of Georgia were debating whether or not to keep the Confederate flag as a part of the state flag. Although this debate had gone on for years, it was heating up as national organizations had threatened boycotts of Georgia and other states that continued to use this symbol. I had introduced editorials and letters to the editor about the topic, and I had assigned a composition that required students to take a stand on the issue.

The papers in general were very good, but Sarah's stood out as one of the absolute best. She, as many white people did at the time, made the claim that the Confederate flag had nothing to do with race, but was a reminder of the Southern way of life. She wrote a paper invoking such a beautiful view of Southern traditions including a paragraph on buttermilk biscuits and turnip greens that would have made any Southerner proud. Race never factored into her views about the flag. Although I didn't agree with her, her paper seemed to me to be incredibly persuasive, no small feat considering my long opposition to that symbol.

John, the sponsor of the newspaper, agreed to do a full two pages on the controversy using excerpts from the papers of my students. I thought this would be a good chance for ninth graders to get to see their names in print. While John only used a couple sentences from the majority of the students' papers, he chose two papers to use in their entirety, one for each side. Sarah's paper was the one he chose to represent the pro-Confederate symbol side.

Sarah did very well all throughout the class, and as time went on, she often came into the classroom in the morning before school to talk with me. I was surprised one morning when I saw that Sarah was at school even before I got there (I always got to school at least 45 minutes to an hour before I was supposed to be there). Sarah knew the route that I normally took to walk to my classroom, and she was waiting for me at the doors that led to the path to my classroom portable.

Since it occurred to me that Sarah had been standing there for some time, it didn't take me long to see that this was no normal visit from Sarah. As we started walking to my classroom, Sarah immediately started a conversation:

"Can I ask you a question?"

"Of course."

"This question is personal."

"Go ahead and ask. If it is too personal, I will tell you that I won't answer it."

"Are you gay?"

"Yes."

"I'm gay too."

"How do you know you are gay?"

Her reply caught me off guard, "Because last night I had a dream, and in the dream I knew I was gay."

Unfortunately, I laughed before I said, "One dream doesn't make you gay. It's fine if you are gay, but people have all kinds of dreams and fantasies, and they can have those dreams and fantasies and not necessarily be gay."

I said all this because something inexplicable about the conversation made me wonder if Sarah was gay or not. I continued:

"Look, you are great, and whether you are gay or straight, to me, you will always be great."

We finished our walk to the classroom, and the rest of the day went on as normal. As I watched Sarah mature over the years, she would alternate between times when she was certain that she was a lesbian and other times when she would be positive that she was straight. At all times I would just reassure her that I cared about her regardless of her identity. When Sarah was a senior, Dryden High School formed its first Gay Straight Alliance, and Sarah was one of the founders. When Sarah graduated, she got a scholarship from the Parents and Friends of Lesbians and Gays (PFLAG).

Sarah could have been accepted by many colleges, but she made up her mind early that she wanted to go to Agnes Scott College primarily because it was a college for women and partially because it was in state. She didn't want to leave the South. While at college, she continued to explore her sexuality and finally met a man and got married. As she told me, "I went to Agnes Scott to find a nice woman to marry, and instead, I found a nice man."

Sarah still stands out in my mind as an example of the fluidity that is possible. It was a reminder to me that we need to allow people the chance to explore all options, and not in any way indicate that somehow one choice is better than others.

NICK

At the same time that Sarah was revealing her struggles with issues of sexuality, another student brought home to me the difficulties that LGBTQ teens faced on other fronts. To be open about being an LGBTQ person at that time was exceedingly difficult. Most LGBTQ students wouldn't have considered it. But there were a few pioneers.

When Janice encountered a new student who came to Dryden on a hardship case because of harassment at his previous school, she asked me to mentor him. I was reluctant because the previous time I had mentored a gay student at Janice's request, it felt like a failure to me. That student was extremely closeted, and no matter how many times I told him that I didn't think that high school, especially at that time, was the safest place to come out, he still felt that somehow I wanted him to identify himself publicly as gay. He harbored a great deal of self-loathing, and nothing I could do would break through to him. We met during my planning periods, and after a while we both gave up.

Nick was very different. He walked in my classroom to introduce himself, and immediately stuck out his hand to shake hands with me. He had incredible self-confidence for someone in the ninth grade. As the year went on, he would frequently come in before school and talk with me. Nick was tremendously smart and good looking. One would think that these qualities should have made him have an easy time at the school. But Nick struggled throughout his time in the public school system. Most of Nick's problems were somehow tied to the alienation he felt because of being gay.

His parents were in many ways very supportive. When he was being harassed at his previous school, they had gone to great lengths to get him moved to Dryden. His parents loved him and were not going to allow him to be bullied. On the other hand, it was very hard for his parents to accept his being gay, in part because of the fact that they were Jehovah's Witnesses. In addition to this, Nick had at times acted out by doing some things that were clearly dangerous, and this gave his parents reason to fear for his choices. His parents were frustrated with the situation, but they were happy to have a teacher mentoring Nick.

Towards the end of the school year, his parents

decided to move to Ohio. Nick would still call every once in awhile and let me know how he was doing. He loved Ohio, mainly because he met his first boyfriend while he was there. His father had tried to be accepting when it came to the issue of Nick being gay, but he couldn't accept the idea of Nick actually having a boyfriend. Making matters even worse, Nick's parents had found condoms in his room. To be fair, his parents would have been upset by this even if Nick had been in a heterosexual relationship. Their religious beliefs forbade premarital sex, and they certainly wouldn't have been happy to find that a teen was contemplating sex. This created a huge argument between Nick and his father.

Nick and his boyfriend felt that they were being wronged by Nick's father. They couldn't accept that this same thing might have occurred if they were a straight teenage couple contemplating a sexual relationship. As Nick and his father continued the argument, Nick's father ordered him to have nothing to do with his boyfriend from that point forward. Naturally, being a teenager, Nick and his boyfriend did the most foolish thing they could think of. They decided to run away.

With the money they were able to pool together, they were able to buy a bus ticket to Atlanta. On one of their stops, Nick called me at school. When he told Mrs. Woods, the secretary, that it was urgent, she got me out of class. Nick told me that he was on his way to Atlanta. When I asked him what he was going to do when he got to Atlanta, he didn't have a plan. I told him that his parents must be beside themselves with worry, and I wanted him to call his father and let his father know where he was. Nick refused. He called back later in the day, and I convinced him to give me his father's phone number so I could call him and let him know where Nick was. I told him to come to my apartment when he got to Atlanta, and I would let his father know that he would be there.

When I called Nick's father, I thought he would be happy to know that Nick was safe and would thank me for letting him know. In my mind I imagined Nick's father getting on a plane and immediately flying to Atlanta to pick Nick up. To my surprise, Nick's father was incredibly angry with me:

"You tell Nick to get off that bus, turn around, and come back here."

"I have no way to get in touch with Nick. I told him to come to my place when he gets to Atlanta. At least that way we will know where he is."

"If Nick goes to your place, I am going to have you arrested."

"Don't you think it would be better to let him stay at my place so you can come get him?"

"No. He can turn around and come back the same way he left. If he gets to your place, I am going to call the police and have you arrested."

"How is he going to get the money to take the bus back?"

"I don't care how he gets the money to come back. He can come up with that money the same way he came up with the money to leave."

"I don't know what you want me to do. I have no way of getting in touch with Nick. I am going back to my class. I'm still teaching. I thought you would appreciate knowing where Nick is."

With that, I hung up. Mrs. Woods, the secretary who

got me out of class, was sitting at her desk while I took Nick's phone call, and she is the one who arranged for me to make the long-distance call to Nick's father, so she had heard much of that phone call as well. She was in as much disbelief about the father's attitude as I was. I had taught her son, and so she knew that I was trying to protect Nick. She told me she couldn't believe how this father was acting. I asked her to call for me if Nick called back, and I would leave class in order to take his phone call.

Much later in the day, Nick called back. I told him about the phone call with his father, but I left out the parts about his father's threats towards me. I did tell him that his father wanted him to turn around and come back immediately. I didn't want Nick to get even more angry with his father and do something even more foolish, so I didn't tell him that his father had no intention of sending him the money to come back. I tried to put the most positive spin on things I could, and I emphasized how much his parents loved him and how worried they must be. I convinced Nick to call his father and at least have a talk with him. I didn't hear back from Nick for the rest of the school day.

Much later that evening, Nick's father called me at home and asked me if I knew where Nick was. When I told his dad that I hadn't heard from him, his father told me about the phone conversation they had earlier in the day. He told Nick to turn around and come back and told Nick that if he went to my place I would be arrested. When I again asked Nick's father if it wouldn't have been better to let him come to my place so at least we would know where Nick was, his father asked me if I intended to let Nick and his boyfriend live with me and support them. I was so incredulous at this irrational way of thinking that I laughed at him. I told him that I had a one-bedroom apartment and wasn't planning on trying to support two teenagers. The conversation went on for thirty minutes or more. I pointed out to his father that if he had followed my plan at least we would know where Nick was. By the end of the conversation, I think he finally understood that I was just trying to give Nick a place to stay so we could keep him safe.

For hours none of us knew where Nick was. Nick's father kept calling me periodically through the night. These calls would alternate between threats towards me and pleas for my help. When Nick finally called at around two in the morning, he wouldn't tell me where he was except to say that he was staying with some gay friends he had met through the internet when he lived in Atlanta. I convinced him again to call his father and chastised him somewhat for worrying everyone so much. Over a period of a few days, his father finally convinced him to come back home.

When Nick returned home, his father cared even less for his boyfriend than he had before. After several months had passed, the family decided to move back to the Atlanta area in part to get Nick away from his boyfriend. When they moved back, they moved to a different suburb outside of Atlanta. Nick went to an alternative school instead of a traditional school so that he could take classes at his own pace and catch up on credits he had missed due to the many school transfers.

Nick wanted me to meet his parents, and we met over breakfast one morning. The father was very polite, and Nick's mother pulled me aside at the end of the meal and thanked me for what I had done for her son. By that time, Nick had a boyfriend who his parents actually approved of. While on a visit to Ohio with his father, he met a young man who was also a Jehovah's Witness, and they started dating. By that time, his father and the rest of the family were so accepting of Nick that his father gave Nick's boyfriend a job in his company. Now that he had a boyfriend, Nick started doing very well in school, and once he graduated, he was accepted at a prestigious university. His parents got an apartment for Nick and his boyfriend in Midtown so that Nick could finish his schoolwork. This was one of the biggest turnarounds I had ever witnessed in working with LGBTQ students, and it showed me that the times really were changing.

KRIS

Without a doubt, one of the most unique students I have ever met was Kris. Kris stood out in many ways. One was his love of writing. He was constantly writing. Even when class was going on, he would listen to what I was saying while filling page after page with writing. These weren't notes; they were personal reflections and fictional stories. This was pretty unusual for a ninth grader in a regular, rather than an advanced, class.

Even before I knew about his love for writing, there was something that made Kris different. The way he dressed, the way he acted, everything about him set him apart from the other students. He had his own group of friends who were completely devoted to him, but like Kris, they were all sort of the "outcasts" of high school society.

After only about a week in the class, Kris let me know that he was born a female, but he identified as a male. Certainly, the idea of a transgender person was not new to me, but this was the first time to my knowledge that I had a transgender student. Strangely, it did make me have to rethink some of the ways that I conducted my class. These weren't major things, and until I met Kris, I hadn't even considered some of them.

One of the customary occurrences that I had to reconsider was the way I greeted students at the door. For years, I stood at the door to welcome the students as they came to class. Years before meeting Kris, I had already had to change one aspect of this method of greeting. While I was in graduate school, during a conversation about the ways we treat males as opposed to the ways we treat females, I had an epiphany regarding my usual greeting of the students when I realized that perhaps I had a certain amount of subtle sexism that I still had not dealt with. I realized that when young men came to the door, I would say, "Welcome, sir." When young women came to the door, I would say, "Welcome," and I then would use the young woman's first name. During the discussion in my graduate school class, I started rethinking this practice. I realized that I was giving the male students a term of respect, while I was addressing the female students in a familiar and informal way. When I brought this up in my graduate class, other students said, "I think it is nice that you refer to the girls by their first name. It personalizes it." The professor, Dr. Albers, disagreed with those students and said, "No. I agree with you. It is sexist. It is giving the males more respect. It is subconsciously giving them more power." From that point forward, I tried to make a point of saying, "Welcome, sir or madam," as appropriate.

Now Kris was making me rethink this strategy as well. Before Kris explained his circumstance to me, I was uncertain myself regarding his gender. While I would greet the other students as sir or madam, I would just say welcome when Kris walked in the door. He must have seen my awkwardness whenever this occurred. Once Kris explained to me that he identified as male, I quickly started referring to him as sir when he entered the room.

What became a little more difficult was a tradition that always took place on Fridays. I tried to make Fridays a little more fun for the students by always scheduling a vocabulary quiz. Of course, vocabulary quizzes on their own are not that fun, so we lightened up the class by playing Jeopardy as a review for the quiz. To increase the fun, we played the men against the women and kept up with the wins throughout the "season." The team that won the most games would get bonus points on the final exam.

I had played this game with the students since my first year of teaching. At first, I had the students pick teams, but I didn't like this practice for a few reasons. My first objection was that the least popular kids would always be chosen last, even when they were often the best students. My second objection was that I noticed in the first few years that the teams almost never chose a girl to be the leader. I knew that if we played the men against the women, at least one girl would have to step up and lead. What I didn't realize until I started dividing the teams by gender was the natural rivalry that took place. Playing the men against the women made the students try even harder than they would have if they had chosen the teams.

With Kris in the class, I had to rethink the way I set up

the game. I knew that he did not want to be on the women's team, but I also knew that the other boys might be rude to him if I put him on the men's team. I also didn't want to bring any attention to the fact that this was even an issue. That year, I went back to my original plan and had the students choose the teams.

I was trying to be very careful not to "out" Kris, but this plan went astray one day when the secretary from the main office called the room. Because Kris' name was gender neutral, students didn't really even think about his gender. However, when the secretary did her very familiar: "Mr. Fair?" I replied, "Yes." She asked, "Do you have Kris in class?" I quickly answered, "Yes." I could see the problem coming even before the secretary said, "Could you send her to the office?" Although the kids did look around the room with a somewhat puzzled look, they still didn't necessarily think that Kris was a girl. They were so accustomed to the office messing up the student's name and other information that they just thought this was one of those commonplace mistakes.

During my planning period, I went to see Lily, the assistant principal. It was probably unfair that I went to Lily about any LGBTQ issues, but I just assumed that because she was a lesbian, she would be more understanding of the situation. Most of the time this was true, but I couldn't have been any more wrong in this particular situation.

After giving her a brief overview of the problem, I told her that it would be best if when calling for Kris, the office staff was instructed to say him instead of her. Lily told me that they couldn't do that because of legal issues involved and said the school might be sued. My response was, "You can't be sued for calling someone by the wrong pronoun, especially if they request it." I went on to say that if they felt uncomfortable calling Kris by a masculine pronoun, they could word their request in a way that was gender neutral. Perhaps they could just say, "Could you send the student to the office?" She said she couldn't do it without parental approval. She did say that she would call Kris' parents and discuss the issue with them which is more than any other assistant principal probably would have done.

As gradually more and more students became aware of Kris' situation, more and more problems occurred. Kris wasn't actively picked on that I know of, but he was shunned by many students. He countered this by spending hours on the internet, which by that time had caught on, especially with the students. This was all going on during the early days of internet use, and AOL chat rooms were the primary source of social interaction on the internet. He met a young woman in a chat room and started an "online relationship" with her. He would spend so much time on the internet with her that his grades started to fall. There was also a concern that he was deceiving this girl about his birth gender.

The social worker was called in, and she decided a meeting was necessary. I always hated these types of meetings because the student was always on the hot seat surrounded by a room filled with adults. This meeting included the social worker, the counselor, the parents, Lily, Kris, and me. I think that I was invited to the meeting because I was the first teacher to bring up these concerns. To my surprise, Kris' parents were two gay males. I would have thought that being gay themselves, they would have been a little more knowledgeable about gender identity issues, but in many ways they were as confused as any straight parents might have been. They were clearly trying to be supportive towards Kris, so at least their hearts were in the right place. Kris' dad started off the meeting by talking about how long this "problem" had been going on. He told a story about Kris' early days growing up and how he would try to get Kris to wear dresses, and he would refuse. He said that when Kris was invited to parties as a child, he would tell Kris that "she" could only go to the party if "she" wore a dress. Kris would choose to stay home rather than dress as a girl.

Any ninth-grade student surrounded by a room full of adults being questioned would be nervous, but in my opinion the social worker made the situation even worse. This social worker was very young, and it was clear that she had never encountered an issue dealing with gender identity. Apparently, they hadn't covered this issue in her master's program either. It was clear to me that this wasn't something Kris was "confused" about. This was clearly the way Kris saw himself, but the social worker kept treating it as if it was a case of "gender confusion" that needed psychological help to be overcome. I got more and more angry as the social worker kept making references to Kris' "problem." I was stunned that the adults in the room couldn't see that it was the school that needed to change, not Kris.

The meeting went on for over an hour, so at the end of the first hour, I saw that I would have to go back to class. I announced this to the group, and I clearly let everyone involved know of my frustration with the meeting. I said, "Kris, I am sorry that this meeting has gone the way it has.

I am sure that we are giving you the impression that something is wrong with you, and I want you to know there is nothing wrong with you. There is something wrong with us because we clearly don't have the knowledge or wisdom to understand what you are going through. You are a great person and a great student and just let me know of anything I can do to help you." With that I left the meeting.

I don't know how much changed for Kris during that school year, but he did make it through the year. He told his online girlfriend that he was born a female, and she was surprisingly accepting of it. He went on to write his poetry and his blogs. I lost touch with Kris when his parents moved to another school system. Although having a transgender student in class was a rare encounter, I was disappointed with the way we all handled the situation. I think we could have done much more for Kris, and I hoped for a day when transgender students would have a better experience in the school system. As educators we had failed to realize that we had put a transgender student in a difficult position. Their school day is fraught with difficulties from where to use the restroom, how to manage the locker room and what to do with the typical teenage attractions they develop for other students. It seemed to me that the least we could do would be to try to make it easier for them.

GAY STRAIGHT ALLIANCE

Every school year throughout the decade of the nineties, Dryden High grew in size. The decade was a prosperous one. Upward mobility seemed to be the order of the day. Bill Clinton was president for most of the decade, and these were the years that Hillary Clinton would later refer to in her campaigns as the years of "peace and prosperity."

The community was exploding in growth, and this suburb of Atlanta was getting increasingly affluent and sophisticated. Gated communities were springing up all throughout the area, and the building of so-called McMansions that were being so discussed nationwide were becoming a commonplace occurrence in the community. In other places of the nation, these large homes were being ridiculed as a conspicuous display of wealth. In this school district, they were welcomed with open arms. Land that had once been farmland was quickly being transformed into estates.

This rapid growth always meant that the school was hiring new teachers. For the most part, getting a job in education requires having a personal connection at the school, and many times these new teachers were hired because they knew someone who was already working at Dryden. Lily and her partner went to a church that was accepting of LGBTQ people, and through this church, Lily met two of the new teachers the school hired for the Talented and Gifted Program. One of these new teachers was the wife of the minister of Lily's church, and the other one was the wife of a minister of a church in the Virginia Highlands neighborhood of Atlanta.

Not surprisingly perhaps, both of these women went out of their way to be friendly to me, and as I got to know them, I learned how much both of them were committed to promoting the cause of LGBTQ rights. One of the two, Jennifer, was in the midst of a controversy regarding her church. The Virginia Highlands Baptist Church had decided to create a statement welcoming LGBTQ members. The Southern Baptist Convention had warned them to rescind the statement or be thrown out of the convention. The ensuing battle over the statement was covered extensively by the news media even on a national scale, and it divided the members of the church. As the minister of the church, Jennifer's husband led the fight to leave the statement in place. The congregation struggled with the decision, but ultimately refused to rescind the statement, and so their affiliation with the convention was removed.

Shortly after Jennifer started working at Dryden, she approached me about her plan to start a Gay Straight Alliance at the school. One of her students in the talented and gifted program had come out to her, and Sarah, the young woman who kept vacillating between being straight and being a lesbian, was also a student in the talented and gifted program. Jennifer wondered if I would like to co-sponsor this group with her. I told her that I would be reluctant to sponsor the group because I didn't want to be accused of trying to "recruit" students into being lesbian or gay. This was a charge often made by anti-gay forces at the time. Talk radio hosts loved to use lesbian and gay teachers as specific examples of how teachers were forcing their values on the students. Jennifer understood my objection, but she wanted to know if I would at least offer advice and attend some of the meetings, and I told her I would be glad to.

Not too long after this talk, Jennifer came to me again to tell me that the administration had refused to allow the group to form, and she had made an appointment with Mr.

Lusk to discuss it. She asked me if I would go to the meeting with her, and I agreed. I was reluctant to go because I had a similar meeting with Mr. Lusk the prior year about a different topic. Agnes Smith, an African-American teacher, had asked me to go with her to talk about the school's talent show. The show often depicted African-Americans in stereotypical ways, and although I didn't attend any of the shows, I had heard from the black students how upsetting this was to them. I went with Mrs. Smith, and Mr. Lusk was receptive. However, since Mr. Lusk was always so supportive of me, I didn't want to be the one who was constantly complaining. Nevertheless, I agreed to attend the meeting with Jennifer.

Jennifer started off the meeting by saying that she wanted to start the club and gave a list of reasons why it was needed. Mr Lusk responded:

"I am generally supportive of the idea of this club. I love the idea that these students will have some support, but we have some very conservative parents here. Many of them would be concerned about having a gay group on campus."

I replied, "You can't really deny the club the right to exist. Under the Equal Access Act, you have to let the students form the club unless you want all the other clubs to shut down."

"Are you saying that every club in the school would have to shut down?" Mr. Lusk asked.

"Not every club. But any club that doesn't specifically focus on a part of the curriculum. You could have a science club or the National Honor Society, but you couldn't have a chess club or the Fellowship of Christian Athletes," I replied.

"Do you have any documentation showing that that's the case?"

"I have plenty of documentation proving that."

"Randy, do you really want to take it this far?"

"Absolutely, I do."

Mr. Lusk asked me to bring him the information about the Equal Access Act, and he said that he would consult the school system's attorneys about it. I brought the documents, and Mr. Lusk consulted with the lawyers.

A few weeks later Mr. Lusk told Jennifer that she could start the club. He asked her to go slowly with it, so as not to cause a controversy. Jennifer agreed to that, and she had no problem getting the club going because the young man who had asked her to start it was very popular at the school. An attractive young man, he was constantly surrounded by a large number of young women who all agreed to be members of the club.

The club went along fine and had a small group of twelve to fifteen members. I attended some of the meetings, and I loaned them my video of the documentary *The Times of Harvey Milk*. I had loved this movie from the first time I ever saw it, and for years, I made every man I ever dated watch it. I should have known that a documentary wouldn't have been appealing to a group of teens, and most of the students in the group didn't enjoy it. The group wanted the club to be less educational and more social, and I could understand the need for that.

As the year went on, the members of the club wanted to reach out to more potential members who might not even know the club existed. Jennifer went to Mr. Lusk and asked him if the group could put up posters as other clubs did and have their meeting times announced over the intercom like the other groups. Mr. Lusk didn't think it was a good idea. He wasn't being homophobic. I think he really supported the idea of the club, but he didn't want to involve the school in any controversies. He knew that the more visible the club became, the more likely it would be to draw parent complaints.

Jennifer kept after him, and he finally agreed to allow both the posters and the announcements, but he told Jennifer she couldn't use the name Gay Straight Alliance. Instead, she could only use the acronym, GSA. Jennifer didn't immediately object to this, but the more she thought about it, the more she disliked the idea. There wouldn't be any point of trying to promote the group if the students didn't know what the group was about.

Jennifer asked for another meeting with Mr. Lusk, and again she asked me to go with her to the meeting. When we got to the meeting, Mr. Lusk immediately took charge:

"Jennifer, I am glad that you are running this group. I really love the idea that our gay and lesbian students have this resource and are getting support. I told you when I let you start the group that there were some parents who were against having this type of group on campus. I want you to think about how you are being allowed to form this group, and I don't want to make any of these parents angry."

I jumped in ahead of Jennifer, "I don't think it's fair to ask the Gay Straight Alliance to use only an acronym. No one will even know what the club is."

"There are other groups in the school that don't use their full name and instead just use an acronym. Look at the FCA. They don't use the full name."

"You can't compare the FCA to the Gay Straight

Alliance. The FCA has been around for years. Everyone knows what it stands for, and the acronym isn't even descriptive anymore. The club now allows students who aren't athletes, and about a fourth of the school belongs to the club. I don't think forcing the Gay Straight Alliance to use an acronym will withstand a legal challenge."

Mr. Lusk looked me directly in the eye, "If you want to continue asserting your legal rights, it might be that someone would want to challenge you, and they might investigate whether this club was initiated by students or by teachers. Under the Equal Access Act, the club has to be initiated by a student."

"I don't fear any investigation of that type."

"Okay. We can end this here. I will check with the lawyers, and Jennifer, I will get back to you."

I don't think he really meant to threaten us, but he clearly didn't like his authority being challenged, and more than that, he really just wanted to avoid controversy. After about a week, he approved the use of the full name of the group. However, he also announced a change in the way announcements would be done in the future.

In the past, we had always had the reading of the announcements over the intercom in the morning and the afternoon. Mr. Lusk said that the reading of club meetings was taking too much time away from class instruction. From that point on, the announcements would be read during study hall by each individual teacher rather than over the intercom. This would ultimately cut down on the number of students who would hear about the Gay Straight Alliance since many teachers would not read the name of the club.

At the same time this argument regarding the

treatment of the Gay Straight Alliance was going on, I got into an argument with Lily over the FCA. A group of students came to inform me that the FCA had just adopted new rules. Under these new rules, officers in the club were barred from "having premarital sex or being homosexual." The news of the new rules was making its way throughout the student body.

When school was over for the day, I confronted Lily about it. Lily was on the front porch of the school because it was her day to oversee the boarding of the buses. The argument we had took place in front of a small group of students, but I went ahead with it anyway. I pointed out how discriminatory this policy was and that discrimination was against the school rules regarding clubs. Lily asserted that the group was not denying anyone membership in the group, only preventing them from being officers in the club. Lily pointed out that the members of the club felt this was consistent with their understanding of Christianity.

I argued that technically the club should be forced to disband because of its discriminatory policies, and Lily nodded that she understood, but pointed out that the new rule had been approved by the administration. Knowing that Lily was a Christian herself, I said, "Wow! Mary Magdalene couldn't be an officer in the Dryden High FCA." A few of the students around us nodded in agreement with me. Lily promised to look into the situation. Again, I realized that it was probably unfair that I was constantly engaging Lily in these battles, but I knew that at least she would listen.

After consulting with the lawyers from the downtown offices, the club was allowed to keep its rules in place. So while the Gay Straight Alliance was effectively being prevented from having its voice heard, the FCA was being allowed to overtly discriminate. Many times in situations like these, I had to realize that although I might try to fight these battles, I would probably lose more of them than I would win.

DISSERTATION

As I got further along in my coursework at Georgia State, my dissertation started to come together more and more. I was very lucky to be at Dryden because the members of the English department were more than receptive to the idea of helping me in any way possible. Over my years of teaching, I had become more and more curious about the way I had seen English teachers approaching the works of lesbian and gay authors. I had wondered why they revealed all sorts of personal information about the life of the authors except in the case when the author was lesbian or gay.

In some cases, it was clearly because the teachers didn't know the sexual orientation of the author. This was in part because the biographies included in the anthology wouldn't include the information about the author's sexual orientation, even in the cases where it was clear that this was a well-known fact that could not be disputed by scholars. I had harped on this fact since the first textbook adoption took place in my early days of teaching.

From that first confrontation with the representative from the textbook company, I continued to point out the discrepancy between how heterosexual authors were treated in the biographies included in the textbooks as compared to how homosexual authors were treated. I pointed out that the spouse of the author was always mentioned in the case of heterosexual authors, but the partner of lesbian and gay authors was never mentioned. The textbook biography would always point out that Robert Frost married his co-valedictorian, Elinor White. However, the textbook biography never mentioned anything about Walt Whitman's sexuality. Some might excuse this because Whitman wasn't committed to a lifelong partner, but that argument could hardly be made when the biography of Gertrude Stein didn't point out her partnership with Alice B. Toklas.

When I brought this issue up with other English teachers over the years, they all had a somewhat similar response to why they wouldn't tell the students even if they knew the author to be lesbian or gay. They said that there was no point in bringing up the author's sexual orientation because the work of art stood on its own. This point of view was consistent with the training that they had received in college. In the time period most of these teachers had gone to school, they were trained in the literary theory of New Criticism which was generally believed to say that a work of art should "stand on its own" and not be understood through its time period or the life of its author. Over the years, I had developed a standard response to this point of view, which was "Why does virtually every high school English teacher tell students that Edgar Allan Poe as an adult man married his teenage cousin?" I could see the argument for revealing this information during the reading of "Annabel Lee," but every English teacher I knew talked about this fact no matter what work they were reading with the kids. It struck me as hypocritical that we could reveal personal information about the lives of straight authors, but we couldn't reveal the same information about gay authors. It also struck me that the marriage of a thirteen-year-old girl to her twenty-six-year-old cousin should be more controversial than the fact that an author was a homosexual.

The more I thought about this discrepancy, the more I wanted to do my dissertation research on why English teachers taught the works of lesbian and gay authors but didn't tell the students that the author was lesbian or gay. My own experiences with my high school teachers, Connie Williams and Billie Bryan, illustrated to me that this could be valuable information for a student to have. Not only did this biographical information empower me as a young, gay man, it also helped me better understand the work.

Knowing that I disagreed with the way most of them were dealing with this information, the English teachers at Dryden were still willing to put in hours allowing me to interview them, observe them, and ask follow up questions. The professors at Georgia State were excited about the topic. Surprisingly, the biggest resistance I found came over my use of the word lesbian. One of my professors, Susan Talburt, was an expert in post-modernism, and she would continually tell me that I couldn't call someone lesbian or gay unless that's the way the person self-identified. While I understood this in theory, for the practical world of high school, this didn't seem to make sense to me. One prominent example illustrated this point:

Elizabeth, one of the English teachers in my study, was

teaching *My Antonia* by Willa Cather. During an interview, Elizabeth stated that she never told the students that Willa Cather was a lesbian because it had nothing to do with the novel. I had not read the novel at the time I did the interview with Elizabeth, so I couldn't dispute this assertion. After the interview, I began reading Cather's work. It struck me as relevant that Cather invented a male narrator, and that our knowledge of Antonia comes from the observations of this narrator. I was also struck by the sheer number of times that this male narrator describes Antonia in masculine ways. Throughout the novel, the narrator tells us that his admiration of Antonia includes such details as her having hands like a man and working in the fields like a man. It seemed to me that this might provoke a classroom discussion of a possible gay reading of the novel.

When I approached Elizabeth with this idea, she insisted that Cather's lesbian identity had nothing to do with the novel. Elizabeth had been one of the teachers educated in the time when New Criticism was the reigning educational theory in literature. Even though Elizabeth spent two class days with her students going over the life of Edgar Allan Poe, she didn't think that Willa Cather's life was relevant to the novel. In the interview with her, she told me that students would see the picture of Cather in the back of the book and would ask if she was a lesbian. The picture in the book was one that depicted Cather in a somewhat masculine way. Elizabeth would tell the students that it didn't matter if Cather was a lesbian and would instead use the picture as a means of talking about women's rights. She would explain to the students the need for women to assert a more masculine identity if they wanted to succeed in Cather's time period. Elizabeth's points were consistent with some of the opinions I encountered at GSU.

It didn't matter to me whether Cather had self-identified as a lesbian. The relevant point to me was that by today's standard certainly Cather would fit our modern-day definition of a lesbian. I didn't think that an esoteric point about post-modernism should override the knowledge that students might get from a more commonplace and straightforward approach. In my opinion, the fact that Cather's significant relationships throughout her life all involved women was enough evidence for a queer reading of the novel. I didn't need visual evidence that these relationships were consummated sexually.

In discussions at GSU, I would point out that in the early 1800s, people who we now identify as African-Americans would have viewed their identity more in terms of whether they were free or enslaved, but that doesn't mean that when we refer to them today that we are inaccurate by calling them African-Americans. After making it through the oral exam process, I was ready to form my final committee. This conflict took quite some time to work out, but eventually my professors were all on board.

My dissertation committee ironically consisted completely of heterosexuals, and they couldn't have been any more supportive. Peggy Albers, the chair of the committee, had chosen to be my advisor because of my topic. In one of the first papers I had ever written on the topic of lesbian and gay issues, Joyce Many had wanted to help me get it published. Joan Wynne agreed to help me at the critical juncture in the process. The fourth member of the committee, Kathryn Kozatis was so supportive of LGBTQ issues that when I was a student in her class, she went on for so long about lesbian and gay concerns that I found myself at times becoming uncomfortable. To find this kind of support in this time period in the state of Georgia was surprising. It took a great deal of courage for these women to agree to participate in a work that could have caused them to become embroiled in controversy. Even though we were beginning a new century, there was still enough animosity towards LGBTQ concerns that any of these women could have found her career in jeopardy by choosing to help me in my project.

A NEW TYPE OF HOMOPHOBIA

As the century was changing, political divisions in the country were becoming more defined and concrete. The 2000 presidential election outcome with the Supreme Court finally deciding the election in favor of Bush illustrated just how difficult it was for anyone in the country to be neutral. At the time, there were news stories about liberals emigrating to Canada because of the future they anticipated under a Bush regime. Many conservatives in the South became even more hardened in their hatred of liberals, especially when those liberals happened to be LGBTQ people.

No one exemplified this change more than the former governor of Georgia, Zell Miller. As governor, Miller had welcomed the Gay Games to Atlanta and had been generally supportive of the LGBTQ community in Georgia.

By the turn of the century, he was beginning his turn from Democrat to Republican. He would ultimately become so enamored with Bush that he would completely turn his back on the Democratic party by giving the keynote address at the Republican National Convention. This was a mere twelve years after he had given the keynote speech for Bill Clinton at the Democratic National Convention. Miller was also speaking out against LGBTQ issues despite his previous support. A similar shift was taking place on the part of many citizens throughout the South.

Just as the South was moving increasingly to the right, the Dryden High administration as a group was also becoming more conservative in its outlook. The Dryden community had always been predominately Republican. However, there had always been room for people of different points of view. As time went on, there were fewer and fewer people on the faculty or in the administration who didn't embrace a traditional, conservative ideology.

One of the causes of this monolithic view on the part of the leadership of the school and the faculty in general was due to the notorious Atlanta traffic. As traffic increased in the Metro area, it became more difficult to make the commute from Atlanta to Dryden. Most of the more liberal teachers and most of the lesbian and gay teachers lived in the city. As these teachers began to retire or change schools, fewer and fewer lesbian and gay teachers were left at Dryden, and it became more difficult to attract teachers from the city to make such a long commute. The one lesbian who was a longtime and respected member of the administration, Lily, left when she was promoted to principal at another school. Other administrators left as well, and the people hired to take their place tended to have a more conservative worldview. For evidence of this outlook, one only had to look at their diplomas from religious schools. Liberty Baptist University diplomas were proudly displayed on the office walls of some of these new members of the administration.

The reduction of lesbian and gay faculty members contributed to the ignorance of these new administrators, as they had fewer and fewer examples of diversity to inform their viewpoint. In my opinion, a new kind of homophobia emerged on the part of the administration. Gone was the overt homophobia I had experienced from time to time in my early career. This new homophobia was much more guarded. Because of the increasing attention the LGBTQ community was attracting on a nationwide scale, administrators knew that they couldn't express their homophobic views as openly as they had in the past without being accused of discrimination. This new homophobia was acted out in ways that were so subtle that at times I couldn't be sure if it existed at all or was just a product of my imagination. I began to believe it might be an internalized homophobia, and the administrators often weren't even aware of the subconscious feelings they held toward LGBTQ people.

The students at Dryden were and had always been overwhelmingly conservative. By this point in my career at Dryden, the students knew even before they were scheduled for my class that I was very liberal, but they also knew that I invited students to disagree with me and that I respected them even when we didn't share the same views. I had taught the siblings of many of these students, and they typically were predisposed to like me from what they had heard from their family members or previous students. I only had a very few students who were openly hostile and disrespectful, and when these students acted out, I saw a reluctance on the part of the administrators to deal with the issue. This reluctance was different from the downright hostility I had encountered with these situations in the past.

A couple of incidents that I had with students that called for disciplinary action on the part of the administration highlighted for me just how uncomfortable this new administration was with any issues involving LGBTQ concerns.

To understand the first incident of this new type of homophobia I encountered, one has to understand the changes going on in the culture at large and the culture of Dryden High with regard to discipline. The difficulties I faced with two young women in my ninth-grade class involved the increasing awareness of LGBTQ people, the increasing comfort level students had with discussions of sexuality, and the increasing use of computers by students.

As computers went from a novelty to becoming almost universally accessible, students were using computers in ways that most adults in the school system were unfamiliar with. Often, the use of social media was blurring the lines between what happened at school and what happened at home. There was a huge push to give students more time and practice with computer use, and at the same time, some students were more skilled with computers than the teachers were. Some students used this greater knowledge to employ computers in inappropriate ways.

At the same time that computers were beginning to be

widely used both at home and in school, schools also were dealing with the lack of inhibition on the part of students with regard to sexual matters. Late in the decade of the nineties, the impeachment trial of Bill Clinton had created a national discussion of sex that changed the very nature of how our society talked about this aspect of human nature. The impeachment trial that took place saturated the society with frank discussions of sexual acts that had been conversational taboos in the time period before. Students knew that Monica Lewinsky's dress was being tested for semen and later understood that this semen belonged to Bill Clinton. Clinton's famous quote, "It depends on what the meaning of the word 'is' is," stimulated a great deal of discussion. Because of this quote, the entire nation was publicly discussing various sex acts and which of these acts constituted sexual intercourse. Not surprisingly, the students were discussing some of the more salacious aspects of the trial. Just as this trial changed the way the news media discussed sexual details, it also made the students more aware of sex and more free to discuss sex in open ways. While the incident with Bill Clinton took place in the nineties, the openness it created trickled down to future generations of students.

This new comfort level with discussions of sex on the part of students also included a greater awareness of LGBTQ issues. Increasingly, even movies and television shows that were created for teenagers included lesbian and gay characters. Unable to discuss these issues openly in class, students often satisfied their curiosity through the internet or by having these discussions with other teens. This often meant that students had no awareness of boundaries when it came to talking about LGBTQ people, discussing sex or sexuality, or using computers in appropriate ways.

Administrators at Dryden typically didn't do well with discipline even when the rules were clear cut, and these vast cultural changes had made it even more difficult for administrators to know how to handle situations that came up that were new to them. This often meant that students got away with things they should have been punished for.

A lax discipline strategy was nothing new for Dryden. It was embedded deeply in the school culture. In fact, Dryden was known around the county for its lenient enforcement of the rules. I had witnessed this from my very first years at the school. Discipline was handled in a completely different manner in this affluent, suburban school than it had been in the mixed-race and less affluent community that Riverside High served.

An incident in my first year at Dryden brought these differences home to me. A scandal erupted when it became public knowledge that the concession stand for the football games was being robbed. The concession stand was staffed by the parents who made up the booster club. On Friday nights when the parents cleaned up and closed the stand, they left the money they had made from the sales during the game locked inside. On Mondays, a parent would pick the money up and deposit it in the bank. This had been the procedure for years and years.

Because the parents' pattern of handling the money was so well known, a group of students started to rob the concession stand each week. In order to figure out who was breaking in the concession stand, the booster parents had a secret camera installed. The next week several seniors were caught in the act of taking the money. They were immediately suspended from school, and the police were planning to charge them with a criminal offense. The students involved were popular kids, and the scandal was all any of the students could talk about.

The parents of all the students accused hired lawyers who notified the school that they would be filing a lawsuit for entrapment. Within days, the suspension of the students was lifted, and all thought of charging the people caught on the tape with a crime was dropped.

This brought home to me just how differently rich kids were treated in comparison with poor kids. I remember thinking at the time that if the same thing had happened when I had been teaching at Riverside, the kids involved would all have landed in jail. Without parents who had the ability to hire high-priced lawyers, these less affluent children would never have been allowed to claim that their rights had been violated.

The lax enforcement of discipline at Dryden was somewhat understandable. The administrators at Dryden were wonderful people, but just as the teachers felt that they were not supported by the administrators, the administrators felt that they weren't supported by their superiors at the downtown offices. Affluent parents would make their voices heard, and no matter how wrong the behavior was on the part of the child, often the parents would have their way.

This failure to address discipline problems could remain hidden from the general public because the demands for special treatment only came from a very small group of parents. The overwhelming majority of parents wanted their children to learn proper behavior, and they supported the administrators' decisions. The more affluent the community became over the years, the fewer discipline problems we had. These affluent parents for the most part insisted that their children get the best education possible. Many of the parents had moved to the area because of the school, and they did not want their children to be involved in any behavior that might disrupt the school day.

However, with a very small minority of the parents, any discipline their child received was too much. For the most part, I had learned over the years to deal with discipline issues on my own. Typically, involving an administrator only made matters worse. However, there were times when students crossed the line in such a severe way that an administrator had to be involved.

One such incident of this type of discipline problem occurred with the two young women I had in a ninth-grade class, Betty and Sue. Betty was a bright, articulate girl who had an incredible ability to write. She was one of my favorite students in the class, but I recognized immediately that her unstable home life was causing her behavior to be erratic. Her best friend, Sue, was a special education student, and her behavior could also be erratic. Although Sue had some problems processing some of the information, she was still a fairly capable student. She had attached herself completely to Betty and would follow Betty's lead wherever it took her.

For most of the year, Betty was a top student. She maintained a high grade, and she actively participated in class discussions. There was a marked difference in her behavior and classroom productivity between the times when her home life was stable as opposed to the times when she was in turmoil. As the year went on, her attendance became increasingly erratic, and when she was at school, she often was understandably far more focused on her problems at home than she was on her schoolwork.

During spring semester, I had the students in the computer lab working on their research papers. I was helping some other students when a few students approached me and warned me that I should look at Betty's computer. Social networking sites were in their infancy at that time, and Betty and Sue had created a page on one of the social network sites. If memory serves me correctly, the site was MySpace. This was the first time I had ever heard of this social networking site. Several of the students had watched Betty and Sue working on the page together. The two had given their page the title "Mr. Fairy." On the page they had made several insulting remarks about me.

I sent them to the office, and they were seen by a fairly new assistant principal, Dorothy. They told her that they did not create the page and said they were merely viewing it. She sent them back to class, and later she told me that there was nothing she could do to prove that they had created the page. When I told her that it should be pretty easy to get the computer specialist at the school to trace the history on the computer, and see if it had been created on that particular computer at that time, she claimed it couldn't be done. When I told her that several students had watched the girls making the page, she wanted me to bring them in to fill out reports. I did not want to drag the students into it, and I could see that even if I did, this woman would do little or nothing about the incident. I came to this conclusion during our discussion when I reasoned with Dorothy that even if we couldn't prove the girls had created the page, they should be punished for being on a site that was not a part of the day's lesson. Dorothy told me that she couldn't punish them for that.

I didn't have any more incidents from the two for the rest of that year, but Betty's home life became even more erratic, and by the end of the year, she had moved and enrolled in a different school. This caused a great deal of anxiety for Sue. When the next school year started, on the rare occasions when I would see Sue in the hall, she would make a point of coming up and saying, "Hi, Mr. Fairy." I would talk to her about it and turn her in to the administrator, but Dorothy would insist she couldn't discipline Sue because she was in special ed. This all came to a breaking point one day when I was on lunch duty. There was an area near my duty station where students would sit and talk when they finished with their lunch. On this day Sue was sitting in the area with some of her friends when she decided to harass me. She started out with the usual pattern saying, "Hi, Mr. Fairy." When I told her to stop, she started yelling, "Hi, Mr. Fairy," every few minutes. Finally, fed up with her and not wanting the other students to see her get away with this behavior, I took her to Dorothy's office.

Frustrated by Dorothy's past inaction, when I got Sue to the office, I bypassed the secretary. I took her directly into the office and told Dorothy in no uncertain terms that if something wasn't done to stop Sue from this continual harassment, I planned to sue the school for sexual harassment. I wasn't angry with Sue. I was angry with Dorothy for failing to address the problem from the start.

The threat of a lawsuit worked because Dorothy then took action. She worked with the special ed teacher assigned to Sue, and they gave her strict instructions that she was not to ever go near me in the future. Sue was upset because she told them that she liked me and didn't want me to be angry with her. She told her special education teacher that she wanted to come and apologize, but by that point, the teacher told her that it wouldn't be possible for her to interact with me in any way. For the rest of Sue's years at the school I never had another incident with her.

However, my relationship with Dorothy was somewhat destroyed by this incident. Of course, she didn't like being threatened with a lawsuit, and from that moment on, she would avoid interacting with me unless absolutely necessary. Once again, I could relate to the experiences of African-American teachers. Often I would hear white people in the school system say of some black teachers, "You better not mess with that one. You will get sued by the NAACP." In the same way, I had to often decide between asserting my rights and alienating people or letting myself be taken advantage of. Like the black teachers, I would have preferred to have the respect of the administrators, but because of what I saw as their prejudice, the best I could hope for was their fear.

Some years later, I had a similar experience with another new assistant principal. This administrator would later go on to become principal of the school, but as an assistant principal he was often ineffective in dealing with discipline problems in general. He proved totally inept at dealing with problems that involved LGBTQ issues.

The particular case that illustrated this ineptness on his part occurred when I started having problems with an

African-American student in one of my junior classes. This was very unusual because the overwhelming majority of African-American students saw me as someone who was on their side. In past years, I had gained a reputation as one of the few teachers who actively addressed racial issues in the classroom.

As with Betty, Antonio also had a very unstable home life. His situation was probably even worse than Betty's had been. His mother was completely inattentive to anything going on in Antonio's life to the point that she didn't even list her phone number in his records. Antonio was frequently absent, and it was impossible to get in touch with his mother when disciplinary issues arose. He had a great deal of anger about things that went on in his home life, and because he was powerless at home, he would direct that anger into classroom situations.

In my class, Antonio started out by making very subtle homophobic jokes. No one in the class would laugh at these jokes, and in many ways, I felt sorry for him. He was already somewhat alienated in Dryden's student culture by his race and his poverty. When no one laughed at his jokes, it merely reinforced his sense of isolation. Instead of stopping this behavior when these jokes were ineffective, he escalated it. By the time we got to the novel Moby Dick, he would say every day, "I bet you like Moby Dick." I spoke to him about it every day for about three days in a row. He continued, but then took it even a step further when he muttered "faggot" under his breath, but clearly loud enough for all the students to hear.

I didn't react to Antonio because I didn't want to interrupt what the class was working on, and I thought I would just speak to him at the end of class. Because he didn't get the reaction he was looking for, he said it very loudly and clearly directed it towards me. When I told him to go to the office, he refused, and I had to call for a resource officer to remove him from class. To the assistant principal's credit, he came down to check on me and make sure I was alright. However, he didn't take any action other than to give Antonio a verbal warning. Antonio came back to class and did the same thing. I sent him to the office again, and again, nothing happened.

When I spoke to the administrator about it, he said he couldn't do anything because he couldn't get in touch with Antonio's parents. I pointed out that legally he had to do something about it. He told me that Antonio was in trouble in many of his other classes also, and that he was working on getting the social worker involved. Shortly after my conversation with the assistant principal, I saw him in Dorothy's office talking with her. I don't know if they were discussing the situation that I had with her years earlier, but I suspected that was the case.

I didn't have to press the issue any further. By this time, the other students had decided to police the situation themselves. They were as tired of Antonio's disruptions as I was. I noticed that when Antonio returned to class his bad behavior had stopped, and I noticed that Blake, a very large football player, had moved his seat next to Antonio. I didn't give it much thought. I was just glad Antonio had stopped the bad behavior. A couple of months later, Antonio withdrew from school. It was only after Antonio left school that I discovered that the students in the class had gotten Blake to threaten him. Blake had told Antonio that if he said anything else about me, he was going to beat him up. The students didn't tell me about this at that time because they knew I wouldn't approve of making threats against the student, but they were tired of having this kid ruin the class for them. I thought at that time that it was unfortunate that even the students could see how ineffective the administrators were when it came to discipline.

Unlike the earlier incidents with administrators over the tardy issues, I didn't think of these two assistant principals as being overtly homophobic. It is quite possible that their refusal to deal with these two students was based on other factors. Dorothy was new at the job, and because the incident involved computer use and a student in the special education program, it is quite possible that she was simply too inexperienced to know what to do. The other assistant principal was dealing with a student who was severely impoverished and a mother who was completely disinterested in her son's behavior or education. It is unlikely that he had ever faced a situation like that in the Dryden community, and it is very possible that he didn't know how to deal with the situation. However, I couldn't help wonder how these ad-ministrators might have acted differently if the comments of these students had been racial epithets instead of homophobic ones. While it was necessary for me to make administrators aware that homophobic comments had to be considered just as egregious and had to be dealt with in the same way as any other pejorative terms towards a group of people, doing so made the relationship between us strained. I never had the same relationship with these administrators that other faculty members did because I had to use threats to make them do the right thing.

Luckily for me, I had the support of the overwhelming

majority of the students. Most of the students at Dryden were overly protective of me, and problems like the ones with these students were relatively rare.

POLITICS AND THE SCHOOL SYSTEM

When I left home on September 11th, 2001, it was like every other day. Living in Atlanta and commuting so far to Dryden, I left my house by 6:45 each day, and although I listened to NPR on the way to school every day, everything on that day seemed pretty normal. I remember that I was paying close attention to NPR because I hadn't picked out an article for the newspaper article of the day. Once I got to school at about 7:15 or 7:20, I was out of touch with any news source because I was focused on getting the lessons ready for my classes.

When school started that day, none of us knew what was going on. The students knew that I loved current events, and a student who came in late told us all that a plane had crashed into the World Trade Center. At the time, we thought it was accidental. Cell phones weren't as prevalent at the time, and the cell phones most students had were not commonly used to connect with the internet.

The news of what really was happening was slow in coming, but by the end of the first period class, the principal made an announcement about what happened. Many parents started to arrive at school to take their children home. There was widespread fear. Many teachers in the school turned on their classroom televisions, and for the students who remained, most of the day was spent watching the news coverage.

By the next day, most of the students were back, but some teachers continued to play the news coverage throughout the day. I could understand why the teachers would do this because it was almost impossible to get the students to focus on anything else. I decided to go on with the day as usual. I felt that it would be more reassuring to teenagers to have the security of a regular routine. Some students felt that I was being unpatriotic, but once I explained my reasoning, most students were ready to go back to work. We would get updates over the school intercom system when anything of significance needed to be reported.

For me personally, September 11th in many ways marked the turning point as far as my participation in Atlanta's gay community went. When the tragedy of September 11th took place, any idea of identity politics seemed irrelevant. With the nation riveted to the news coverage, for a brief moment, our identity as citizens of the United States trumped any identity we might have had because of our race, ethnicity, gender or sexuality. The politics of the tragedy of September 11th took all the steam out of all other political issues. When the moment passed, it became much more important whether a person was a warmonger or a pacifist.

Even before the tragedy of September 11th, national politics were becoming more prominent for the average citizen than they had ever been before. Because of the controversy surrounding the Supreme Court decision making George Bush president, discussions of politics were front and center at dinner tables around the country. This meant that students who were typically uninterested and uniformed about political issues suddenly became interested in ways that they hadn't been in the past.

At Dryden High, this meant that overwhelmingly the students supported Bush, and their support became almost a part of their identity. Suddenly, students began placing Bush bumper stickers on their books, bookbags, and cars. The white W with the black background was ubiquitous. Bush t-shirts became popular with a large segment of the student population. This affinity for Bush became even more pronounced after the September 11th attacks. As we began Bush's War on Terror, the students, like the overwhelming majority of the country, completely supported Bush's policy.

The newspaper article of the day activity that had been a standard for my class and was somewhat popular, now became something even more well-loved by the students. Now, large numbers of students were interested in and eager to discuss the events of the day. Because of the high interest on the part of students, it was easy to get them engaged in almost all current events.

Ironically, the discussion that caused the most controversy that year was the one I was least expecting to be controversial. The article I had chosen was about the clothing store Abercrombie & Fitch. The store was being sued for discrimination. Several members of minority groups had charged that they had been offered jobs in the back-stocking shelves, but were not allowed on the sales floor because they didn't have the "Abercrombie look."

One of the most volatile discussions that I had ever conducted in all my years of doing this activity broke out. Perhaps I should have realized that this particular brand had become at that time almost synonymous with a certain identity, but the truth of the matter was that I was totally unaware of the clothes the students were wearing because I knew nothing about fashion.

Many of the white students wore Abercrombie & Fitch clothes and so strongly identified with the brand that any criticism of it became personal to them. These students were adamant that Abercrombie & Fitch should be able to exclude anyone who didn't have the look the company was trying to promote.

Several members of minority groups in the class were just as adamant that the students who wore the brand were not only racist but were classist as well. These students pointed out that these clothes were worn at that time almost exclusively by white people. Often, the students who couldn't afford these clothes thought that the affluent white students who wore Abercrombie & Fitch were doing so to set themselves apart from other students and to assert their advantaged status.

As the conversation went on, some students took the comments so personally, that a couple of them started crying in class. After the class, some students went to the assistant principal to say that the article had caused too much controversy. Dorothy, the assistant principal, came down to ask me about what had happened. I explained the situation, and she asked me to stop using the article for the rest of the day I told her that I would continue to use the article and explained that just because something was controversial or caused a passionate response that was no reason to stop using it. I continued to use the article throughout the day, and although the comments continued to be passionate on both sides, the students handled it well, and there were no further issues.

I didn't encourage controversy in my classroom, but I

didn't shrink from it either. This put me at odds with the administrators. From my experience, it seemed that many administrators didn't want any controversy to ever occur. Some administrators would be fine with a lesson that was dry as dirt because it made their job easier. The students, on the other hand, wanted to have lessons that challenged them and brought out their passionate opinions and ideas.

As the Bush years went on, the students had many opportunities to engage in passionate discussions about current events. As the country debated the impending Iraq War, students were eager to share their feelings about whether the mythical "weapons of mass destruction" actually existed. Students gave their opinions on whether we should go to war and whether other countries should support us in this war. Feelings were especially strong when France refused to join with the U.S. in the war. These feelings were perhaps at their most ludicrous level when people renamed French fries and instead called them freedom fries. Students were able to have discussions about all of these topics, and while they were often passionate about their opinions, none of these discussions caused the type of controversy the Abercrombie & Fitch discussion did.

As the 2003–2004 school year started, many of the teachers, no matter what subject they taught, were getting into a playful banter with the students about the upcoming primaries. Just as in the 2000 election, many of the students were displaying an interest in politics that went way past what students had demonstrated previously. Suddenly, W stickers were everywhere, as the over-whelming majority of students still supported Bush.

Evidently, parents must have complained about

teachers discussing the election because shortly after the election year started, the faculty got several emails warning us that we weren't allowed to talk about the election in class. These emails always threatened us with dismissal. At the time I thought again, "So much for not abandoning your first amendment rights when you 'enter the schoolhouse door." I chose to ignore these threats, and I continued my newspaper article of the day activity. I knew that since this was part of the normal curriculum for my class, I was well within my rights to have this as my opening activity.

Naturally, during an election year, many of the newspaper articles of the day concerned the upcoming election. Although most of the students were Republicans, the small minority of Democrats enjoyed taking on the ideas of their classmates, and both sides of the discussion would get passionate about their political beliefs. Nevertheless, the students were able to air their differences without too much controversy. I felt that the discussions were valuable and added to the students' understanding of what was going on in the world. In addition to the awareness of current events, the students also gained in their ability to support the arguments they made. No one ever complained about any of these discussions.

While none of these election year discussions caused me any problems, the newspaper of the day activity brought controversy in 2004 when President Bush refused to let reporters show the photos of the flag-draped coffins of returning dead from the war in Iraq. The controversy surrounding this decision was in the news for weeks, and I did a series of newspaper articles of the day on it. After this, there were many articles concerning the number of soldiers who lost their lives in the war, and I used several of these articles as well.

Far from being controversial, I thought the articles in question were among some of the most patriotic things I had ever done in the classroom. These stories were major headlines at the time, and while they were about a controversy that was going on, I didn't think my use of them was controversial. My team teacher at the time had a son who was serving in the military, and she appreciated the articles about the sacrifice that military members were making. Many times she would comment about our need to have respect for the troops that were risking their lives for their country. A couple of students in the class felt that the articles made them feel bad because they became sad about the deaths of these young women and men, and they would rather not think about the war.

I first found out that there was a controversy about the articles when the teacher across the hall asked me if I knew that Chuck, an assistant principal, was standing outside my classroom each day listening in. I hadn't known it. I had a long-time policy of keeping my classroom door open when at all possible because I knew that some people were suspicious of a gay teacher, and I didn't want them to think I had anything to hide. I found out later that Chuck had been standing outside my door because a parent had called to complain. The parent took exception to the articles about the returning coffins. The parent said that by talking about the fact that the press was not allowed to show the coffins of those killed in the war, I was upsetting the students and trying to convince them to be against the war. The parent had promised that he was going to make me "famous all over the country" for presenting a biased view of the war.

Chuck called June, the department chair, in and told her that he had listened in, heard the discussion, and knew that I wasn't being biased. Despite the fact that Chuck knew nothing inappropriate was being said by me, he asked June about the possibility of me no longer presenting the newspaper article of the day. June insisted that this activity was sound practice, especially since the writing topic on the SAT at the time required students to write persuasive papers. She insisted that the activity should continue and that we shouldn't back down over a single parent. Chuck called the parent and assured the parent that I was not presenting the articles in a biased way and that I was giving the students a chance to air whatever views they might have about the subject. He also pointed out to the parent that my team teacher had a son in the military and completely supported my use of the articles. He offered to move the student to another teacher's class, but the parent didn't want that. For a period of about two weeks, Chuck continued to monitor my classes periodically from outside the classroom door. When the parent continued to complain, Chuck told him to take whatever action he wanted because he would not ask me to stop the activity since it was consistent with proper pedagogy. The parent dropped his complaints, and I never heard another thing about it.

Far from being angry about the newspaper article of the day, most parents over the years complimented me on having that as part of my class. Frequently, parents would say that at dinner they would ask their child what the newspaper article of the day was, and then the family would have a discussion about the topic. I think the parents were glad to have their children learning about current events and developing an opinion on those events. Moreover, I think they were even happier to have a topic that they could discuss with their teenage child. Many parents told me over the years that when their child became a teen it became increasingly difficult to have conversations. This activity gave them an automatic source of discussion. I made the "article of the day" a standard activity throughout the remainder of my career.

GUEST SPEAKER

Shortly after September 11th, my dissertation was finished, and I was ready to defend it. My defense couldn't have gone more smoothly. As my defense took place, I was surrounded by professors and spectators who were completely supportive. This could have easily gone the other way. Not only was my dissertation about LGBTQ issues in education, it also was based on a method that went against the research that was current at the time.

When I began to plan my study, I had originally wanted to achieve the kind of praxis Paulo Freire describes in *Pedagogy of the Oppressed*. I was drawn to Freire's idea of engaging people in their own process of overcoming oppression. However, I quickly realized that wouldn't work for my study. I was using the English teachers at Dryden as my participants, not the LGBTQ students who were being oppressed. Moreover, the English teachers I used in my study, for the most part, had little interest in LGBTQ issues as they applied to the teaching of English.

This had put me in a bit of a dilemma.

I totally abandoned any sense of the neutrality that is often an aspiration for a researcher. Instead of merely recording the feelings of my participants, I carried on a back and forth dialogue, challenging the participants to think more deeply about how they approached the work of LGBTQ authors.

A typical exchange would go something like this:

"Do you tell the students that Langston Hughes was gay?"

"No. It doesn't have anything to do with the poetry."

"Do you tell them Langston Hughes was black?"

"Well, of course. You can't discuss the poetry without telling the students that he was black."

"What do you think the difference is?"

I would do this with a host of examples challenging teachers to look at the way they treated lesbian and gay authors differently.

The most contentious of these interviews took place when I interviewed Lily, the lesbian assistant principal. I had decided to include Lily for the study because prior to being an assistant principal, she had taught English. Lily was insistent that being lesbian or gay had nothing to do with the works, so she saw no reason to bring up the sexuality of the authors. I used several examples to illustrate ways that the identity of the author did matter. When I got to the works of Walt Whitman, I recited directly from the textbook, "I am enamored of growing outdoors, / of men that live among cattle or taste of the ocean or woods, / of the builders and steerers of ships, of the wielders of axes and mauls, of the drivers of horses, / I can eat and sleep with them week in and week out." I pointed out that those lines usually provoked the students to ask me if Walt Whitman was gay. I pointed out that LGBTQ students might benefit from being told Whitman was gay because it might provide the role model of a well-respected gay man, and straight students would benefit by having their stereotypes challenged. After this exchange, Lily gave me the title for my dissertation when she said, "No, I wouldn't [tell the students that an author was lesbian or gay], and yes, I probably should."

Rather than being bothered by the fact that my interviews were more of an argument than the traditional and customary approach by a neutral observer, the professors loved the method I had chosen. Kathryn Kozatis was effusive in her praise, telling me that I had created a new method of research. When the dissertation was complete, some of the professors at Georgia State started using parts of it in their classes. This was more of a tribute to the English teachers who participated in the study than it was for me. Most of these teachers had taught for twenty years or more, and the conversations I had with them were rich in raising issues, not only with regard to sexuality, but with regard to race, ethnicity, gender and other issues of identity.

Not long after receiving my Ph.D., a woman who had gone through the doctoral program with me called me. Lee Daily was now working as a professor at Georgia State, and she was teaching a class called "Literature for a Diverse Society." She had decided to devote a class period to LGBTQ issues in the classroom. As a student at Georgia State, I had been a guest in Peggy Albers' class when she had been discussing LGBTQ issues. Dr. Albers had praised my participation in that class, and Lee had heard about it.

Lee invited me to come in and speak to her class on the day that she had set aside. Lee's class was a master's level class filled with teachers who were ready to do their practicum work and then begin teaching. I was thrilled to have a chance to raise the awareness of teachers with regard to LGBTQ issues.

This started a period of years when once a semester I would give these talks to the students taking this class. When Lee no longer taught the class, Susan Crim McClendon, took over the class, and she also invited me to speak. For all of the many years I spoke, every semester at least one member of the class would tell the professor in charge that they would not attend class on that day because of religious or political reasons. I never minded this, but I did worry about students at a university who couldn't bear to hear anything that conflicted with their own already established ideas.

I would start the class by sharing letters I had received from students over the years telling me of the ways I had changed their lives. I would also talk about Connie Williams and Billie Bryan, the high school teachers who had changed my life.

After the initial stories about my teachers, I would use the rest of my time on questions from the audience. It never failed that one of the first questions I would be asked was whether I thought my being gay was genetic or was a choice. The answer I gave was never what the person asking wanted to hear. I would tell them that I did think that it was genetic, but that I wished the LGBTQ community wouldn't argue it that way. I told them that if I could have chosen being gay I would have, and that I thought the LGBTQ community should argue this issue from the point of view that we should have the freedom to be who we want to be, not the argument that was so prevalent—that we couldn't help it.

I didn't like the genetic argument for a couple of reasons. The first reason was that the genetic argument was based on a premise of LGBTQ people as victims. I would tell the class that this argument bothered me because I was proud to be gay, and I didn't view it as something that couldn't be helped. I would go on to explain that the other problem with this argument is that I felt we would "win the battle, but lose the war." While I knew that eventually the genetic argument would prevail, I felt that the LGBTQ movement was at its best when it expanded the idea of people being free to choose. I felt that once we won the argument based on genetics, other people who wanted to live their lives as they choose would be hurt rather than helped by our newfound freedoms because only differences that were genetic would be honored.

Two other questions that always came up in the classes were also ones that found me on the opposite side of most in the LGBTQ community. Students in the class always asked about whether LGBTQ people should be allowed to marry and to serve in the military. Again, I had to explain that I wanted LGBTQ people to have the freedom to do anything they wanted to do in society; however, I couldn't on a personal level see why they wanted to do these two things. The sodomy law was still the law of the land, and I couldn't see why people would want to fight and possibly die for a country that made their very existence illegal. In the same way, I worried about the marriage law. It seemed to me that LGBTQ people were fighting to be more like heterosexuals, and the greatest gift that LGBTQ people have brought to society throughout our existence has been the ability to expand people's ideas of how to live a life of individuality and difference.

Most of the questions the students asked were specific to school rather than these larger political questions, and I was able to answer their questions using examples from my own experience. After I had spoken each time, the professors told me that some of the people who had been most reluctant to stay for the class had been the ones who said they enjoyed it the most. I wasn't worried about changing any of the students' minds with these classes. I was just happy the conversation was taking place at all. Many of these students expressed that they had never had this topic discussed in a class before.

One of the most disturbing of the questions that I ever had during these class speaking sessions occurred in Susan Crim McClendon's class. Susan was a very intelligent and beautiful African-American woman. She was somewhat of a star at Georgia State. Besides her own intelligence, she also had a degree of fame. Her father became the first African-American school superintendent of any large Southern school district when he was named the superintendent of Atlanta Public Schools. A floor in the education building at Georgia State was named in his honor. Susan's husband and both of her sons were football stars.

Because of Susan's fame and intelligence, she attracted a large number of African-Americans to her classes. The classes that Lee taught were often majority white, but Susan's classes sometimes were as much as three-fourths African-American. There was a stereotype at the time that

African-Americans were hostile to LGBTQ rights. This stereotype was in large part based on the importance of the church in African-American culture. Oftentimes, LGBTQ people would assume that black people automatically felt that LGBTQ people were sinful. Studies at the time often showed that African-Americans were less likely than whites to support LGBTQ rights.

My own experience with African-Americans did not support these findings. More often than not, I had found that African-Americans were often very supportive. Some of the major leaders of the civil rights movement had been among the first to speak out in favor of LGBTQ rights. Coretta Scot King, an icon of the Atlanta community, had been very vocal in her support. Joseph Lowery, the president of the Southern Christian Leadership Conference, had faced down detractors when he said that he had suffered too much bigotry in his life to ignore prejudice faced by other groups of people.

These conflicting views of the LGBTQ rights movement could easily be observed in the classes I spoke to. From time to time, African-American students in the class would object to any comparisons I made to the black civil rights movement. They would often say that I shouldn't compare the two movements because black people were part of a culture and LGBTQ people couldn't be said to be a cultural group. My time in Dr. Winston's class had prepared me to counter this point of view, but more often than not, the person who asked the question would still insist that there was no LGBTQ culture.

More often than the argument about culture, the statements and questions of the students reflected deep religious conflicts in people's feelings towards LGBTQ people. Many of the African-Americans in the classes would say that they wanted to support LGBQT rights because they understood what it felt like to face discrimination, but their church taught that homosexuality was sinful.

Frequently they would quote the Biblical injunctions against homosexuality. I would always respond by saying that people's personal and religious views should not have anything to do with the way students were treated in schools. I would also caution the students about using Biblical justification for discrimination and would point out to them the fact that during the times of slavery Southerners would point to the passage, "Slaves be obedient to your masters," or tell the story of Paul returning the runaway slave to his master in order to support their belief that God wanted slavery to exist.

None of these comments surprised me because I had heard many of these arguments for years. The moment that did shock me was when one of the students brought up his feelings about a homophobic attack that had taken place at Morehouse College.

I probably shouldn't have been surprised because many of these same arguments had taken place in the media. The story had been major news in Atlanta from the moment of the attack in 2002 through the trial in 2003. Aaron Price, a student at Morehouse, a historically black private college, had beaten another student, Gregory Love, nearly to death with a baseball bat because he thought that Love had been looking at him in the shower. Later it turned out that the victim was actually straight, but at the time, the perpetrator, the son of a well-known African-American preacher, used gay panic as his defense.

Because this attack had saturated local news, I wasn't surprised that it came up in the conversation, but I was startled by the way one particular student approached the topic. He asked me what I thought about the case, and I made some general comments about the state of our society when a student at one of the most prestigious colleges in the state could be attacked and nearly killed by another student. The man who asked the question, an attractive African-American man in his early twenties, responded to my comments by saying he didn't know what he would do if another man looked at him in the shower. He implied that he might do the same thing.

I responded to him by asking what would happen if every woman who had ever been looked at inappropriately by a man thought she was justified in killing the man. I suggested that there might not be a lot of heterosexual men left in the world and went on to say that women in our society are almost expected to accept being objectified.

The man insisted that men looking at women was "normal," and that he wouldn't want another man looking at him in the shower. Other African-American men in the class started making comments in support of this man's opinion. In many ways their fears mirrored the arguments people were making at the time about the possibility of LGBTQ people serving in the military. Many politicians at the time were making the case that LGBTQ people couldn't openly serve in the military because members of the military had to be in close quarters with each other.

To counter these arguments, I told the class the story from my high school experience of Connie Williams telling our class about her lesbian roommate and told them of her response to students, "I'm comfortable with my sexuality, so if a woman looked at me and thought I was beautiful, I would be just as happy as if a man did." I then asked them if these fears they had about gay men didn't represent their own insecurities about their sexuality. There was a shocked silence in the class as many of these men reflected on these thoughts, but I continued taking questions, and for the most part, the rest of the class was similar to other classes I had spoken to.

Another instance that surprised me during my time as a guest speaker at these classes involved the receptionist on the floor where most of the classes met. I had known this woman since my days taking classes for my master's degree. I became curious when I noticed that each time I came to speak to the classes she would no longer allow me to proceed past her desk as I had for all the previous years. Instead, she would go get the professor to escort me to the class. I assumed that this was due to the increased security precautions that had been put in place after the September 11 attacks. But I noticed that it wasn't just the procedure for getting to the class that had changed. Her demeanor towards me seemed different than it had in the past.

I had not considered the fact that she probably only learned that I was gay when I started the guest speaker sessions on the topic. On one of my visits to speak, she asked me if she could sit in on the class. She told me that the professors had already given her permission as long as I also agreed. I told her that I would love for her to sit in. During the talk she asked me several questions of a religious nature and added that she would always believe that homosexuality was a sin. After the talk was over, she stayed to talk to me. She told me that she wanted me to know that she had been against my being allowed to talk about this topic, but now that she had observed the class, she thought that the discussion was fine. I thanked her, but I secretly wondered why she would think I would need the approval of the receptionist to speak when I had been invited by the professor.

Although there were a few instances of resistance, for the most part all of the students in the classes were receptive to the idea of better serving the needs of LGBTQ students. As the years went on, people were so accepting that it seemed as if the days when these talks were needed had already passed.

SODOMY LAWS AND SOCIAL ACCEPTANCE

For forty years of my life and sixteen years of my teaching career, I was a criminal for simply being who I was. Far from hurting me as a teacher, I think this fact actually helped me. In every school I taught in over the years, the students grew to accept me. More often than not, the homophobia I experienced in the school system came from the adults. I think that being gay actually helped my relationship with the students because I think it made me better able to relate to their problems and concerns.

When NPR did an interview with a national teacher of the year during one of my later years of teaching, I better understood something that I had just instinctively known. The teacher of the year made the point that students watch to see how the teacher will treat the weakest student in the room. If the teacher picks on the weaker students, the other students will realize that the teacher can't be trusted and at any time could turn on them. If the teacher defends the weakest student in the room, the other students will know that their areas of weakness won't be used against them.

Because of my identity as a gay man, I think I always identified with the members of minorities, the outsiders, the alternative students, and the withdrawn and socially awkward types. I think that I brought an empathetic quality to my classroom, and I believe that more often than not, the popular and more secure students appreciated the concern I had for all my students. While I think that the marginalized students were happy to have someone who accepted them for who they were, I think that the popular students were also glad to know that their acceptance wasn't dependent on their popularity.

From the beginning of my career, I knew that I had to do something to help the students who didn't fit in. I was determined to stop the bullying that I witnessed almost from the moment I began teaching. After thinking about it for a while, I came up with a strategy that I used for almost twenty years. I had read an article in *The Atlanta Constitution* about a student, Brian Head, who had killed himself. I knew the article would be particularly poignant because it was about something that had taken place on the local level at a high school that the students would have heard of. Brian Head was a student at Etowah High school in Georgia. For years the students had used a nickname for Head that referred to his weight. This had been going on for so long, that most of the students thought nothing of the name. Head brought a gun to school intending to kill the students who had been bullying him. His best friend got between him and the students he intended to shoot. He shot his best friend by accident, and in remorse for having shot his friend, he turned the gun on himself. This was 1994, long before school shootings had become commonplace. The article hit home with my students because they could relate to Brian's classmates. Many of the students interviewed for the article said they wondered if they might have contributed to Head's death because of their frequent use of the nickname he had been given years before his death.

This article was also relevant because most of the bullying I witnessed in my early years of teaching had to do with weight. I decided to use this article on the first day of class because I knew that in the adolescent male mind once a derogatory word was uttered, the male who was a victim of the taunt would immediately want to retaliate. This typically would become a spiral that would only end when the verbal assaults were replaced with physical assaults. The article worked pretty well with the students, and on the occasions when someone crossed the line, I could always refer to the article when I spoke to the person about the offensive behavior.

As the years went on, and the nation became more aware of LGBTQ people, I saw increasing bullying on the basis of sexuality. At Dryden, I was constantly nagging the administrators about the gay slurs that often appeared on lockers, walls, and bathroom stalls. At one point, I took a camera to school and took pictures of all the gay slurs on lockers, in the restrooms and on the walls of the stairwells. I then showed the pictures to the administrators who had told me that the problem was not as bad as I was making it sound. It was hard for them to continue with that argument when they were confronted with photographic evidence.

After I wrote the column about Matthew Shepard, I combined it with the article about Brian Head and used them both on the first day. I wanted to tamp down the homophobic comments before they could even get started.

For most of my teaching career, I taught what were called "on level" or "regular classes." These classes were for the students who weren't ready for honors or advanced placement classes, and these were the classes where the bullying of others was most likely to take place. I had requested to teach the "on level" classes because I felt that they were the most oppressed students in the school. I think this could in part explain their tendency to bully others because they felt belittled by their place in the school system.

I quickly saw that at Dryden there was hierarchy to the school culture, and what we had was really two schools sharing one building. The students in the honors and advanced classes were almost exclusively in the higher-level classes for most or all of their classes. Typically, they had been in these upper level classes for years, and because their friendships were formed in these classes, they usually had very few friends from the "on level" group. Many of the upper level students looked down on the lower level students.

Each year when the students voted for the "Senior Superlatives" for the yearbook, the overwhelming majority of the students who won would be from the honors and advanced classes. The rare exceptions to this were the on-level students who were involved in athletics. The students in upper-level classes voted as a block and that prevented any on-level students from winning. There was also a vote for favorite teachers, one male and one female. For years, these teachers were inevitably the teachers of the honors and advanced classes.

Sometime around the late nineties, I won the award for favorite teacher. I was shocked and honored. Every year with my "on level" classes there was a small but significant number of the students who harbored a great deal of homophobia, and I had to work throughout the year to gain their trust. Not only did I take this award as some validation of my own work with these students, I felt that it was a victory for the other gay and lesbian teachers and a victory for all the teachers who also exclusively taught the on-level group. After that first year, I started winning the award every year. From time to time, the yearbook sponsors would ask me to let them give the award to the person with the second most votes so that other teachers could have a chance at the award.

This popularity with the students did not translate to the adults in the school system. There were always a large group of teachers, parents and especially administrators who felt that LGBTQ people shouldn't be teachers. Most of the time, this message was delivered in very subtle ways, but at times, it could be very overt. When the article about Matthew Shepard was published, other teachers reported to me that the home economics teacher had been very vocal that it was inappropriate for a teacher to write a column that dealt with gay issues. Some teachers made it a point to avoid me. This wasn't atypical for LGBTQ teachers in the South during this time period. In nearby South Carolina, the Republican party platform stated that openly gay teachers should be barred from teaching. In his campaign for Senate in 2004, Jim DeMint stated his support for this part of the platform, and as late as 2010 he reiterated that position. So, it wasn't all that surprising to me that some of the members of the faculty felt that I shouldn't be allowed to teach.

For as many detractors among the adults, I had an equal number of supporters. Many times, these supporters went out of their way to confront those who they thought were treating me unfairly. June was unrelenting in her defense of me, and so were many of the parents. In fact, the parents at Dryden were some of my most steadfast supporters.

In my mind, there was a clear turning point in this hostility I sometimes got from the other faculty members, and it was the year the sodomy laws were struck down by the Supreme Court, 2003. It is hard to imagine that this would have made such a difference, but the change in attitude was palpable. It was almost as if the adults in the school system needed this validation by the government before they could accept me. Teachers and custodians who had never spoken to me before suddenly started greeting me in the mornings. The news changed me as well. Even though I still could be fired for being gay, at least I wasn't branded as a criminal just because of who I was.

The overturning of Bowers v. Hardwick was especially exciting in Georgia. It was the Georgia case that had upheld the sodomy laws in 1986. That case had been a particular thorn in the side of LGBTQ activists in Atlanta. Now, in 2003, less than twenty years later, the infamous case had been overturned. An impromptu gathering at Outwrite Bookstore brought hundreds to celebrate. We had hoped, rather than believed, that this could be the outcome, and now we were legitimately citizens of the United States who couldn't be jailed at the whim of some legal entity.

My life as a teacher changed that day. I knew that now I really was a member of the community, and the change in the other adults at the school made me realize that many of them felt the same way I did. Whether it was the Supreme Court decision or simply the gradual change in culture would be impossible to say. But that day was definitely a symbolic marker. Suddenly, I was no longer a criminal in the eyes of my country of birth.

DAY OF SILENCE

Even though the culture was improving greatly in the area of LGBTQ rights, especially for me as a teacher, that didn't mean that there weren't still problems. And as always, still most of these problems were caused by the adults in school, rather than the students. One of these problems concerned the Gay Straight Alliance Club.

After the initial start of the Gay Straight Alliance Club, I had very little involvement with it. When Jennifer, the woman who started the club, went to another school, there were always straight teachers who were interested in sponsoring the club. I still felt that it was more effective to let a straight teacher sponsor it in order to avoid the charge that there was some kind of recruitment going on. Even though times had changed, I didn't want to even give the slightest impression that I was doing anything untoward.

There had been little flare-ups of controversy over the years, but the students in the group seemed to work through these issues pretty effectively on their own. The students had maintained a small club for a few years, and in the later years most students in the school knew of the existence of the club.

During the 2002–2003 school year, the club, following the lead of the national GLSEN group, decided to participate in the National Day of Silence. Prior to the actual day, the members of the group asked for commitments to participate from both students and teachers. I agreed to participate of course, and I made plans to have the students write an essay on that day that they would have written at some point anyway. I had decided to go with an essay so that the participants on the Day of Silence wouldn't feel the need to speak.

When some of the parents called in to complain, they were careful to make sure that they couldn't be charged with homophobia. They said that their concerns involved their fear that having some students and teachers not speaking would disrupt the school day. They also stated that students who didn't want to participate might feel forced to go along with it since so many other students were participating. The administration at first reacted by canceling the Day of Silence. When students insisted that they had a right to carry out the activity, the administration responded by telling the teachers that they could not participate in the activity. The students were allowed to distribute their handouts explaining why they didn't want to speak on that day, but they were instructed that if called on in class, they had to answer. The day went on without incident. Even if most of the students didn't support the cause, by this point the Dryden student population had become pretty accepting of other people's beliefs and ideas.

As the years went on, the Day of Silence continued with varying degrees of participation, and I never heard of any other problems or controversies associated with it. As LGBTQ people became more accepted by the society, the club had dropped in size perhaps because not as many students felt that they needed it.

During the 2010–2011 school year, the president of the Gay Straight Alliance was a student in my class. That is when I first heard that the school had made them change their name to the anti-bullying club. The administrators had told them that by only working on issues involving LGBTQ students, the club was exclusionary and violated the rules set forth by the school system. Interestingly, the school didn't tell the FCA that they were exclusionary because they only accepted Christians as members.

Rather than fight this action on the part of the administration, the students simply accepted it. During the spring, when the time for the National Day of Silence was approaching, the students submitted their plans for the day. The administration told them that they couldn't pass out their handouts that explained that the day was intended to bring attention to the bullying that LGBTQ students experienced in school. The students were told that instead they had to make the handouts more general and address all types of bullying.

I wanted the students to learn to fight their own battles, but I did offer advice when one of my students asked me about the actions of the administrators. Patty, the president of the club, was angry. She had gone along when they had made her change the name of the club, but she didn't want to go along with the change in the Day of Silence. I let her know that she didn't have to give in to the administration's demands. I told her that if she contacted Lambda Legal Defense, I was sure they would contact the school on her behalf. Patty was an advanced placement student, and like many good students, Patty didn't want to be seen as a troublemaker. She told me that she talked with the sponsor of the club and the sponsor encouraged her to go on with the day as the administration wanted.

Despite how far we had come in the issue of LGBTQ rights, this incident showed me how far we still had to go. The administration of the school was still willing to intimidate students working in the area of LGBTQ issues. I don't know that this was necessarily overt homophobia on their part. I think it is more likely that they were still just thinking that they didn't want to deal with anything that might cause controversy and make parents angry.

A NEW CONFIDENCE

Over the years, one of the most heartening things to watch has been the transformation of LGBTQ teens. When I first started teaching, it was virtually unheard of, at least in the South, for a student to "come out." Lesbian and gay students in the 1980s and even in the 90s almost always had a sense of shame and a sense of victimhood. They were always tentative in revealing their homosexuality and always very careful in who they chose to tell.

Over the years, I saw this gradually change. I first noticed this change in students through a new openness in students' writing. Students had come out in their writing through the years because they knew that I wouldn't share this with the other students. But the number of students doing this increased exponentially. Students began to illustrate a point by revealing that they were gay. For example, before the Lawrence versus Texas decision in a paper arguing for the legalization of marijuana, they might say, "Of course the government says it should be illegal, but I'm gay, and the government thinks that's illegal too."

As more students began to be comfortable with their LGBTQ identity, other students started to show more and more support. Increasingly, heterosexual students would not tolerate homophobic comments on the part of their peers.

In one of our Rhetoric Friday debates, we read an editorial regarding whether toys should be gender free. Many students defended the "innate" choice of certain toys for boys and others for girls. An equal number of students argued that children should be free to choose whichever toys they wanted without regard to gender stereotypes. When a male student said, "I would be embarrassed if I had a son that wanted to play with dolls," other students immediately took this to be a veiled reference to some kind of underlying homophobia. One student asked this young man, "What if your son turned out to be gay?" As conservative as this student was, he immediately responded, "If my son turned out to be gay, I would go on loving my son. He would be my son." While this might not seem to be that radical of a statement now, in my experience, that type of statement in a classroom situation would have been unheard of twenty years before.

Even more surprising to me were the times in the last years of my career of students "coming out" in class discussions. One of the first times I ever witnessed this happen was surprisingly during a discussion of how the students might improve their essays. I was going over a set of papers I had just graded, and I told the students that if they wanted a good score on a persuasive essay they had to refute the other side. One of the students asked me if this was really necessary. The student said, "If I make my points strongly enough, what difference does it make if I even mention the other side?" The only analogy I could think of on the spur of the moment was a football one. I said, "Think about football. You might feel that you are the best receiver ever, and you might be, but if you get knocked down on the line of scrimmage, you won't be able to catch the ball. I want you to knock the other points down before your opponent even gets a chance." Immediately, a male student, Mike, who sat in the front of the room said, "I am sorry. I don't get this analogy. Can you make it about hair or makeup?" The entire room erupted in laughter, but it wasn't a malevolent laughter. It was more that they were all in on the joke with Mike, and I wasn't. Most of the students in the class had gone to school together throughout elementary, middle, and now, high school. They had known Mike for years.

I still didn't know if Mike was gay or if he was just making a joke. However, as the class went on, I not only realized that Mike was gay, but I also realized that the other students knew and didn't care one way or the other. This is not to say that Mike didn't experience some difficulties. There was a short period during the year when he told me that some kids were harassing him. But when I tried to get him to tell me who they were, he just said they were "jerks," and there was no reason to do anything about it. These weren't students who were in classes with him. It was very obvious that the other students in the class liked him and accepted him. I could tell that, for them, Mike's being gay was the equivalent of him having brown hair. It was just another fact.

Another student, in a different class that same year, struck me as drawing a very similar reaction from the other students as Mike did. From the very start of the class Cecilia drew awe from the other students for her intelligence. I would sometimes use her essays as examples for the class, and her comments were always filled with insight and were surprising for their maturity. During our Rhetoric Friday discussions, Cecilia and a few of her friends who sat together would verbally spar with a group of students who sat on the other side of the room. This division was a clear conservative/liberal split on the part of the students, and although sometimes anger would flare up, the students seem to handle the debates well.

During one of these Friday debates, Cecilia was responding to the more conservative group and said, "Well, I am a feminist lesbian, and I think everyone in here is responding based on their ideas of gender normative behavior. We should be questioning our stereotypes about gender. Just because I was born with a vagina doesn't mean that I am necessarily going to think or act a certain way." Much of the class was shocked by her comments, but Cecilia was not one to worry about what other people thought or care whether or not they were able to keep up with her intellectually.

She continued to speak up throughout the year, and while some students didn't like her point of view, they didn't harass her about her sexuality. I saw no evidence that she suffered any repercussions by identifying as a lesbian. In fact, if anything, it helped her solidify friendships she had already formed, as those students seemed to be determined to show her support.

During that same year, there were other lesbian and gay students who didn't choose to make their sexuality public knowledge. One of these students, an extremely popular young man, came to me just before he graduated. He had a girlfriend during the time that he took my class, but he wanted me to know that he was bisexual. He said that it had meant a great deal to him to have a gay man for a teacher. I was surprised by his comment since I had no idea that he was bisexual. It was a reminder for me that while there were students like Cecilia and Mike who were completely comfortable asserting their sexual identity, there were even more students who were still reluctant to speak about this aspect of their lives. While we had made great strides in the school system, it still was not a completely comfortable place for some LGBTQ students.

A NEW HOMOPHOBIA?

After I had been teaching at Dryden for about 17 years, two new members of the leadership team were named. I sensed immediate hostility from them. It's difficult to know what is going on in someone's mind, so I never could be sure whether this was homophobia or not.

The first incident that made me wonder occurred at the end of the first year with Abigail and Paris in charge. They both had made a huge point of the fact that during the post-planning days we would need to organize the book rooms because of the sloppy way teachers had returned the books. Because I had time during my advanced placement students' testing days, I cleaned up the book rooms. At our next meeting, Abigail gave a lecture about the need to put the books up correctly in the future, and then she told the other teachers that they wouldn't have to use the post-planning days for this activity because "a little fairy cleaned up the book rooms this year." She continued with her lecture, and two more times during her speech she said, "a little fairy cleaned up the book rooms this year." Each time she made this statement, she would look at Paris and smile.

Both of these teachers suddenly started, in my opinion, to reveal an extremely conservative persona that I had never witnessed before. In the teacher's lounge they began exchanging Christian novels with one of the teachers, and they began talking a great deal about these works. Of course, there was nothing wrong with them engaging in book talks about a topic they were interested in, but then they ordered everyone in the English department to all give the same grammar test. From the first test, it was apparent to me that the sentences used as examples for the test contained a definite political stance. The first test used the following sentences:

1. In the course of an average day, people rarely stop and think about their own country and its flag.
2. As we lead our busy lives, the citizens of this country often overlook their hard-won personal freedom.
3. In school our teachers work to teach about the events of our early history, which help us understand the burning issues which led to the

American Revolution.

4. Since 1775 many men and a growing number of women have made the ultimate sacrifice for the freedom we now enjoy.

5. The Revolutionary War and the Civil War were fought on our own American soil to preserve freedom at home.

6. Other wars were fought to preserve the freedom of people in other countries.

7. Every single day in America, lawyers, law officers and judges struggle to protect the freedom won in many desperate battles.

8. Our much-criticized politicians spend their entire working lives seeing that this huge, complicated country runs smoothly and that our freedom is preserved.

9. Many students have family members who have served their time in the military protecting and preserving America's freedom.

10. Perhaps when we say the Pledge of Allegiance, it is our way of thanking the many dedicated people who have struggled for the freedom we enjoy.

I didn't make any objection to the clearly conservative nature of these sentences because I was accustomed to the overwhelming conservatism of faculty members in every school where I had taught.

It was only after Paris began to discuss my teaching abilities with my former students that I realized I might have some problems. These former students brought this to my attention. I asked them why they would be wasting time talking about me, and they said that Paris had wanted to know if they thought I was a bad teacher and asked them if they thought the assignments I gave were juvenile. One of the students said, "I am sorry I did this, but I have to worry about getting accepted to college. I don't want to hurt my chances. I thought you were a great teacher, but I could see that she wasn't going to let us out of there without us saying something bad about you, so I just started making things up." Louise, one of my favorite students from the previous year, was also questioned. She said, "I don't care what she does. I wasn't going to say anything bad about you, and it made me mad that the other kids did." I told the students not to worry about it, but I reiterated that I didn't think they should be wasting time discussing me.

After this incident, I encountered several other situations with these leaders that I thought bordered on harassment. I asked for a meeting with the two of them and the administrator in charge of English. I pointed out to them that 92% of the students in the previous year's class had scored a three or better on the advanced placement test, making them eligible for college credit. Over forty percent of the students had scored a 4 or 5. I pointed out that for well over twenty years, I had nothing but glowing evaluations from administrators, previous department chairs, parents, and students. They simply remarked, "At Dryden we have higher standards than colleges do." I couldn't help but laugh at this comment since I had taught at Dryden so many years and was very familiar with the standards of the school. On several occasions throughout the meeting, Paris would lean towards me and ask, "Randy, don't you think you are a little too sensitive? Aren't you just a little too sensitive?" I couldn't help but wonder what would happen if a male administrator had said that to a female employee.

In my opinion, some of the other teachers also seemed to be acting differently towards me. Most notably was a teacher named Betty. Betty had always made it a point to let us know that she was a member of the John Birch Society. I had always liked her even though I thought her views were a little strange. Thinking that the school's Young Republican Club was not conservative enough, Betty started a John Birch Society for the students. This was totally her idea, and even though this club was not created by students, no one challenged it as they had the Gay Straight Alliance. Despite our different points of view, we got along well together.

I had taught Betty's daughter in one of my AP classes, and as a professional courtesy, I had gone out of my way to accommodate her daughter's needs. The year I taught her daughter, Betty couldn't tell me enough times what a great job I was doing. The next year, suddenly in department meetings, Betty started making disparaging remarks about my class. When she did this, it would surprise me. I would think to myself how complimentary she had been in the past. As with Abigail's comments, I didn't attribute these comments to homophobia until another incident took place that made it clearer.

In 2012, Chick-fil-A had been in the national news when its COO, Dan Cathy, made comments opposing same sex marriage. After it was revealed that the chain supported anti-gay groups, LGBTQ activists called for a boycott, and counter protestors rushed to eat at the chain in order to provide support. In our school system, we always had an annual meeting of all the English teachers in the county. At this time, these meeting took place in the southern part of the county, a good distance from where most of the teachers at Dryden lived. As always, I got to the meeting early, and to my surprise Betty was already there. I was talking to another teacher when I saw Betty, and she made a point to interrupt our conversation to let me know that she got to the meeting early. I said, "That's great, Betty." She replied, "Yeah, I got here early. I got here so early that I was able to stop off at Chick-fil-A and have breakfast." She put such an emphasis on Chick-fil-A that I couldn't help but take it as a homophobic comment, and when I didn't react, she said it again, "Yeah. I had plenty of time to stop by Chick-fil-A."

As time went on, I felt that I was becoming paranoid, seeing conspiracy everywhere in the department. But my feelings seemed somewhat validated when my former student, Mike, came in to tell me about something that happened in a class taught by Paris. The class had read *Pride and Prejudice*, and on Valentine's day, Paris' assignment was for them to make a Valentine card for one of the characters. The idea that seniors were spending an entire class period making Valentine's cards was disturbing enough to me, but it was Paris' response to a question from a student that had angered Mike. One of the students asked if the students were allowed to make a card for someone of the same sex as them. According to Mike, Paris responded, "Absolutely not. If anyone does that, the person will be referred to the office for disciplinary action." I suggested that Mike go and talk to her and explain how he felt, but Mike feared that talking to her about it would just lead to retaliation. I knew Paris too well by that time to refute his assertion. I also knew that there was a different way to see this. Paris may have made this statement because she wanted to preempt students from treating the assignment as a joke.

As all of these incidents began to add up, one of the college English teachers who offered a class at the school came to me and told me that while she was in the English office, she had overheard Paris tell some of the English teachers that she was "going to take care of me." Whether this was true or not, it was shortly after this time that I started receiving bad evaluations for the first time in my career. One of these evaluations was so ludicrously unfair that I went to the principal to complain. The next week he came to my class to observe and wrote a glowing evaluation where he said the complete opposite of what the other administrator had said.

The next year, Paris completely changed my schedule and the schedule of the other teacher who taught advanced placement classes with me. She gave me what she viewed as a less satisfactory schedule, and when the other AP teacher complained about the change in her schedule, according to this other teacher, Paris told her that she couldn't teach those classes because she was friends with me. When a new administrator was hired, his first reviews of my class were negative also.

It was at this point that I realized that I needed to transfer to a different school. I was three years away from the end of my career, and I knew that I couldn't endure three more years of the harassment. I worried about the possibility of a change because over the years many of the administrators had asserted that no other school in the county would want a gay teacher. Years earlier when I had applied for a transfer, June told me that at a meeting of the department chairs for the county, the chair for that school had asked her if I was "that radical" she had heard about. June replied, "If you mean is he an activist, yes, he is." I thought it would be very difficult to get any school to take me, but through the help of my friends Amy and Ben, I got two offers.

By this point, some of my suspicions about what had gone on at Dryden seemed to me to be confirmed. The new administrator who had given me the original bad review went back and changed it to a positive one. When I met with him about it, he indicated that Abigail and Paris had convinced him that I was a bad teacher. The rest of his reviews were good, and on the last observation of the year, he came back three times to tell me that the class he observed was the best class that he had evaluated the entire year. When I told him that I would be transferring at the end of the year, he apologized for Paris' behavior and said three times, "This is my fault. I need to work with her to help her get better."

CRYSTAL SPRINGS HIGH SCHOOL

If I didn't believe that Dryden High was steeped in homophobia before I left, I certainly did once I got to Crystal Springs High. The experience was as different as night from day. Like the early years at Dryden, Crystal Springs had many lesbian and gay teachers who were completely out to the faculty. More importantly, there were numerous LGBTQ students who were completely out to everyone at the school. I was completely amazed at how open and accepting the school was. The student body was far more diverse ethnically than Dryden was. About a third of the school was white, a third Hispanic, and a third black. I am not sure if this diverse student body was responsible for the difference in the tolerance towards LGBTQ people that was so evident in the school or if it was some other factor.

From the moment I got there, the faculty rushed to make me feel that I was a part of the school community. The first week during lunch there was a great deal of discussion about LGBTQ students. This topic continued to come up during our lunches for a few months. I realized later in the year that the English teachers were bringing up the subject to make me feel more comfortable at the school. A lesbian English teacher went out of her way to let me know that Crystal Springs was a safe place for an LGBTQ teacher. Another English teacher surprised me by the way he played with gender. He was what is sometimes referred to as a metrosexual. He was extremely good looking and very popular with the students. Although he was straight and married, he frequently joked about what a girl he was, and he frequently laughed with his students about his femininity as well. When students would ask him if he was gay, he would respond by saying, "The jury is still out. A lot of people think I am, but my wife doesn't think so." This was clearly a different school climate than what I was accustomed to.

After I had been at school about two weeks, the other AP Language teacher was waiting on me at the end of the school day. He started walking out to my car with me and said he had something to ask me. He was the yearbook sponsor, and one of his yearbook students was also in my AP Language class. He told me that Emma wanted to fix me up with her mother, and he said that he didn't know what to tell her. I told him that if he didn't feel comfortable with the situation, he could just say that it would be unprofessional of me to make a date with a student's parent. Then, I said, "If you feel comfortable with it, just tell her the truth." He said he would like to tell her the truth, and I assured him that would be fine.

The next day, Emma and her friends were whispering together before the class started, and I could tell that I was the subject of the conversation. I could tell that after the initial conversation, the students were fine with it. Just as they had at Dryden, the students started online searches of me, and from tim=e to time they would ask me if I had been a writer for the *Southern Voice*. They would tell me that the comments about me on *ratemyteachers.com* were good and made them laugh. This seemed to make them feel more comfortable with me. After a couple of months, Crystal Springs was much more comfortable to me than Dryden had been despite the fact that I had taught at Dryden for twenty-one years. There just was no sense of hostility or conflict towards me, and in some ways, I didn't know what to make of it.

When time for observations came, the department chair, and the assistant principal in charge of English, gave me very positive reviews. The assistant principal observed me during one of the Rhetoric Friday discussions that Paris had such a problem with. As she left the room, she told me how well she thought the lesson had gone. Later in the year, the other AP teacher told me that he had been at a conference and several teachers started asking him to explain Rhetoric Friday. At first, he didn't know what they were talking about. He said that after a while he realized that the assistant principal had told them had told them about the lesson she observed and had praised it as something they should try to implement in their class.

The entire administration was completely supportive of what I was trying to do in the classroom. After the first month or so, the principal would stand with me in the hall from time to time as I greeted my students. Each time she came over, she would ask me if I was happy at Crystal Springs and if there was anything she could do for me.

In fact, the only real problem I had at the school that first year came from a student who happened to be a lesbian. This student, Josey, was militant from the start. On the first day of class I heard her tell a friend, "I don't think we are going to be able to destroy this class like we do in all the others." Although I didn't know it at the time, Josey had a lot of "demons" that she was pretty open about. She also had a precarious situation at home. These two problems converged when her mother refused to let Josey see a therapist because she feared that Josey's problem would prove to be genetic. Since the mother refused to take Josey to the doctor, Josey was not receiving the help that she desperately needed.

Without that help, Josey had wild mood swings that were completely unpredictable. On the good days, Josey could participate to the fullest because she was one of the brightest students in the class. On the bad days, Josey became one of the most belligerent students I had ever faced in all my years of teaching. I noticed early on that any time I chastised Josey, she became irrationally angry with me, but even angrier with herself. When I would ask her to step into the hall to talk, the anger frequently turned to tears.

One day when we were in the hall, and Josey's anger turned to tears, she said to me, "It isn't you. I just get so angry sometimes. You can't imagine what it's like in the school to be black and a lesbian." I awkwardly hugged her, and it probably was one of the few times she had been hugged by an adult in her entire life. The class only had a few minutes left, and I asked her to look up the name of the woman who wrote the two quotes I had up in the front of the room. For many years, I had two quotes by Audre Lorde at the front of my classroom. One of them said, "I have come to believe over and over again that what is most important to me must be spoken, made verbal and shared, even at the risk of having it bruised or misunderstood." The other said, "When I dare to be powerful, to use my strength in the service of my vision, then it becomes less and less important whether I am afraid." I noticed that Josey had her phone out and was looking up the quotes. At the end of the class, Josey told me that she really liked what she had read about Lorde and wanted to know more.

That night when I got home, I ordered a copy of *Sister Outsider*. After I gave Josey the book, I noticed that every day she carried the book to every class all throughout the day. Frequently, when teachers put her out of the class for her bad behavior, she would sit in the hall reading the book. Josey asked if I could get her other books, and I was only too happy to comply.

This isn't to say that Josey's behavior got any better. If anything, it got even more volatile as the year went on. I spent many planning periods in the office of the counselor. The most surprising thing to me was the counselor's steadfast support. I often voiced to her my concern that Josey had never received unconditional love and that I wanted to make sure that even when I corrected Josey's behavior that I didn't send the message that I didn't like her. The counselor concurred with that. I could understand my own desire to help, but I was heartened by this counselor's efforts. Most people in the school, both students and teachers, disliked Josey. It amazed me that this straight woman would care so much and work so hard for a student who continually acted in defiant and militant ways. As frustrating as it was to work with Josey, the counseling staff's non-judgmental attitude toward her only increased my love of this school and my opinion that times really were changing.

As I left for the summer break that first year, I felt that my experience at Crystal Springs was a complete success. This was confirmed for me even more when, during the summer months, I got an email from the man who took my place at Dryden. I had heard about this man earlier in the school year from my friends at Dryden. A couple of months into the year he was apparently already telling students and teachers that he was planning to leave. From what I heard, he was being harassed even more than I had been in my final years at Dryden. Apparently, he realized that if he quit, the school system could pull his certificate for failure to fulfill his contract. He decided that rather than quit, he would wait it out and make the administrators fire him when they gave him his midyear review. Whether this really was his strategy, I couldn't really say, but he was let go at the end of the first semester. That summer, when I received an email from him, he was in the midst of preparing a lawsuit. He wanted to know if I had experienced any homophobia at Dryden. While the administrators didn't know it when they hired him, it turned out that he was gay.

I started typing an email to him, and I stopped. My past experiences had made me leery of putting anything in writing. I was unsure whether I should answer the email at all. I was now two years away from retiring, and I wanted to totally forget about Dryden High School. I called the assistant principal at Crystal Springs and asked her what she thought. She said, "You know Randy, when I observed your classes this past year, I noticed that you have a poster in your room with a quote from Dante, 'The hottest places in hell are reserved for those who in times of great moral crisis maintain their neutrality.'" Her comment reminded me that over the years I had increasingly started playing it safe. Because I was so far into my career, I let things go that I would have never let go in my earlier years as a teacher. She said, "I will never understand why you didn't file a complaint about the way you were treated at Dryden." She also told me that I should have a talk with the teacher who was filing the suit and said I would find out quickly whether I wanted to help him out or not.

When I called this man, and he described the homophobia he felt he had experienced, he somehow blamed it all on the principal. It turned out that in addition to having a teaching degree, this man was also a lawyer. I told him that I would testify to what had happened to me, but that I didn't think the principal was homophobic. I told him that the principal had wanted me to stay, and that it was the other school leaders who seemed homophobic. He insisted that all of the people had been homophobic in their approach to him. Because this man was a lawyer, I realized that this man would probably settle his case out of court as so many teachers who had been harassed by administrators had done in the past. I thought the system would attach a non-disclosure clause, so that no one would be aware of the settlement. I felt that it was exactly as the book I read by Karen Harbeck so many years before described. Whether this man did win his case, I never heard. But it did give some support to my belief that much of what I experienced in the final years at Dryden could be attributed to homophobia.

TRANSGENDER STUDENTS

Nothing proved to me how much times had changed more than the way transgender students were treated at Crystal Springs. Every year I was there, there were several students who were very open about the fact that they were transgender. The administrators went to great lengths to accommodate the needs of these students. Even before transgender bathroom rights became a part of a national discussion, the administrators at the school made arrangements in advance for these students. Each year before school started, the administrators would meet with the students who identified as non-binary or transgender and make sure that they had a bathroom choice that would be comfortable for them.

During the summer months of the last year I was at Crystal Springs, I received an email from a student who would be in my class in the fall. This student had included all of the teachers for the upcoming year in the email and explained to us what a non-binary identity was and affirmed this identity. The student explained that we should avoid pronouns and gave us the proper name we should use, which was different from the birth name. The name we were to use was not gender specific. The birth name was a very traditionally feminine name. I was impressed by this student's introduction to us, but I was even more impressed that the email included links to various sites that would give us more details on non-binary identity.

This worked with virtually every teacher in the school, for the most part. I will admit that even though I tried to be careful, I had occasional slip ups. For me, even though the student identified as non-binary, my past socialization that had created the habit of dividing the world into male and female was hard to overcome. As much as I tried to see this student as non-binary, to me the student looked very feminine. As much as I did try to avoid pronouns, on a few occasions, I did use the pronoun she. On the few times I did use a pronoun to refer to the student, I apologized later. I think the same was true for almost all the other teachers on the schedule for that year, but there was one prominent exception.

One teacher, who was new to the school but an experienced teacher, announced on the first day of class that she would not allow the use of any nicknames and would only refer to the students using their legal name. The student who identified as non-binary was in her class. When thinking about the situation in retrospect, I had to wonder if the teacher developed this policy only in reaction to the email the student had sent. Of course, the non-binary student had a huge issue with this situation because of the overt gendering that would result by use of the legal name, but other students in the class found the policy objectionable as well. When the students objected, the teacher insisted that it would be too confusing for her to have one name on the class roll and another name that she would use in class. Some students insisted on writing their nicknames when they turned in assignments. She gave all the students who didn't use legal birth names zeroes on the assignments. When parents complained, she told the parents that it was a simple mistake caused by the discrepancy between the name on the paper and the name as it appeared in the grade book. She asked parents how she could possibly give credit if the two names didn't match.

At that point, I was in charge of the new teacher program at the school. Any teachers who were new to the school, whether they were experienced teachers or not, were a part of the program. An administrator asked me to talk to this teacher about some of the problems she was experiencing, including the problem of the students' names.

When I met with this teacher, she again insisted that she could not be expected to remember both a legal name and a nickname, and that the use of one in the grade book and one in the classroom would make it impossible for her to enter grades. When I pointed out to her that I had never had a problem because I simply used last names to input grades and the nickname should have no impact on that, she still insisted that she was obligated to call the student whatever name was in the grade book, in this case the legal birth name. I pointed out to her that I had been in a meeting with her that included the parents of a student who used a nickname. I reminded her how upset the parents were when she refused to use this student's nickname, and I explained that to the parents it seemed that she didn't care enough to get to know their child. This teacher insisted that using nicknames would somehow be illegal, and she fervently believed that parents were trying to persecute her for her refusal to use anything other than a legal name.

While this teacher's insistence on only using legal birth names was disrespectful to all her students, the harm went even farther for some students. By refusing to use the non-gender specific name that the non-binary student preferred, the teacher was causing this student harm on two levels. Every time the teacher called this student the very feminine birth name, she created harm on a psychic level by reasserting a gender that the student didn't recognize. In addition to adding to the confusion the student felt on a mental level, the teacher also created confusion among the student's peers by associating this student's non-gender specific persona with a definite feminine identity. While most of the student's teachers had done a similar thing at some point when we would slip up and use a pronoun, this was different from the teacher who actively refused to carry out the student's wishes.

Fortunately, the administration at Crystal Springs did not take this lightly. After my talk with the teacher, the assistant principal followed up with a meeting of her own. The administrator went over the issue of names and other issues that had come up during the year. Not willing to drop her objections, the teacher decided to leave Crystal Springs and teach elsewhere. Once again, the administration at Crystal Springs had shown that every student mattered.

RETIREMENT

By the time my thirty years of teaching high school had passed, I was uncertain whether I wanted to leave or not. This was a dramatic change from earlier years of my career when the constant battles seemed so overwhelming that I couldn't wait to get out. Now, that feeling had completely passed.

The climate at Crystal Springs High School was largely responsible for this change in my attitude. Many times when people would ask me about Crystal Springs, I would tell them that for me this was teacher paradise. Every day at Crystal Springs I would stand in the hall and marvel at the sea of students hurrying to class. Here was what I always believed could be the best thing the United States had to offer.

The halls of Crystal Springs were filled with students from all racial backgrounds and religious creeds who for the most part got along with each other. Frequently I would see students of different races holding hands as they moved past towards their classrooms. A few of the male students wore yarmulkes every day. Some of the female students wore hijabs. Many of the LGBTQ students felt very comfortable about being completely open to the point where sometimes same-sex couples would even hold hands. Most of the students didn't wear the most expensive clothes available as they had at Dryden or compete with each other to see who could have the most expensive car. Homeless students often were friends with some of their peers who came from the most affluent families in the area.

This isn't to say there weren't problems. Occasionally,

fights did break out. Sometimes these fights even had a racial/ethnic component to them. These fights brought local news coverage because the media loved to present a story that people were eager to believe. However, these cases were exceedingly rare, and the school population at large did not hold animosity towards other groups of people.

Even more challenging at times for teachers was the economic diversity of the school. Teachers at Crystal Springs had to constantly be prepared to support students who might be going through difficult times. The help needed by the student could be emotional or financial, but it was certainly different from the situations I had encountered when teaching at Dryden. Because many of the students at Crystal Springs didn't come from affluent homes, their needs were often far more complex when compared to Dryden.

These complex needs were constant at Crystal Springs, and they could be very draining, but as tiring as it could be, it felt more rewarding to me than any teaching situation in my thirty-year career. At Crystal Springs, I had finally gone from being the gay teacher to being a teacher who happened to be gay. I was part of the school community in a way that had not been true at any of the other schools where I had taught. Even more exciting for me was the fact that at least in this particular school there was no place for the homophobia directed towards students that characterized so much of my other school experiences.

ABOUT ATMOSPHERE PRESS

Atmosphere Press is an independent, full-service publisher for excellent books in all genres and for all audiences. Learn more about what we do at atmospherepress.com.

We encourage you to check out some of Atmosphere's latest nonfiction releases, which are available at Amazon.com and via order from your local bookstore:

Peaceful Meridian: Sailing into War, Protesting at Home, nonfiction by David Rogers Jr.

SEED: A Jack and Lake Creek Book, a novel by Chris S McGee

The Pretend Life, poetry by Michelle Brooks

Rags to Rags, nonfiction by Ellie Guzman

Shining in Infinity, a novel by Charles McIntyre

What?! You Don't Want Children?: Understanding Rejection in the Childfree Lifestyle, nonfiction by Marcia Drut-Davis

GLLU Boy and the One Saving Grace, a novel by William Waxman

Heat in the Vegas Night, nonfiction by Jerry Reedy

Evelio's Garden, nonfiction by Sandra Shaw Homer

Difficulty Swallowing, essays by Kym Cunningham

Gathered, a novel by Kurt Hansen

ACKNOWLEDGMENTS

I want to express my appreciation for all the people at Atmosphere Press who contributed to this book, especially Nick Courtright and Sarah Schuster.

I would like to thank all the people who helped support me throughout my life and throughout this process. This includes all my family and friends. A special thanks to Mike McVey, Gregg Holloway, Anthony Ricciardi, Sharena Hall, Fran Soloman, and Ben Crosby. I would also like to thank the teachers in my life: Judy Hammack, Lisa Ethridge, Noel Quentin, Jackie Angel, Amy Fargusson, Deborah Wells, Nancy Goodyear, Manning Harris, Greg Poulos, Jane Davis, Susan Durden, Geraldine Warren, Ross Friedman, Carly Plonka, Lauren Paine, Vicky Ferguson, and countless others. A special thanks to Gregg Holloway and Vicky Ferguson for providing feedback throughout the process and to Noel Quentin for the quilt included on the cover.

I would like to express my admiration for all the activists who helped make Atlanta a safe space for LGBTQ people. Some of these activists are Anthony Ricciardi, Steve Scarborough, Mona Love, Jeff Graham, Marty Avant, Judy Kolb, Sarah Lynne Chesnutt, Barbara Budd, Collin Quinn, Stephanie Swan, Linda Wilson, Judy Gerber, Chris Crain, and Phillip Rush.

Thank you to Brian McNaught for getting me started on this journey through his book *A Disturbed Peace*.

ABOUT THE AUTHOR

Randy Fair is originally from Weaver, Alabama. He attended undergraduate school at Jacksonville State University where he earned a Bachelor of Science in Education with a concentration in Language Arts. After moving to Atlanta and beginning his teaching career, he attended Georgia State University where he  earned a Masters of Education degree in English Education. He returned to Georgia State where he earned a Specialist of Education degree in English Education and Doctorate in the Philosophy of Teaching and Learning. His essays and writings have appeared in *The Southern Voice*, where he was a regular columnist, *The Houston Voice, The Atlanta Journal, The Anniston Star, Etc. Magazine* and in the anthology, *Telling Tales Out of School*. He is the co-founder of the Atlanta Chapter of the Gay, Lesbian, Straight Teachers Network and was named one of *The Southern Voice* "Twenty-five Who Made a Difference." He is a National Faculty - Smithsonian Fellow, and he taught English for 30 years in the Atlanta area.